A Long and Bloody Task

THE ATLANTA CAMPAIGN
FROM DALTON THROUGH KENNESAW MOUNTAIN TO THE CHATTAHOOCHEE RIVER MAY 5-JULY 18, 1864

by Stephen Davis

EMERGING CIVIL WAR SERIES

Chris Mackowski, series editor
Kristopher D. White, chief historian

Also part of the Emerging Civil War Series:

A Long and Bloody Task

THE ATLANTA CAMPAIGN

FROM DALTON THROUGH KENNESAW MOUNTAIN TO THE CHATTAHOOCHEE RIVER MAY 5-JULY 18, 1864

by Stephen Davis

EMERGING CIVIL WAR SERIES

SB

Savas Beatie

California

First edition, first printing

ISBN-13 (paperback): 978-1-61121-317-1
ISBN-13 (ebook): 978-1-61121-318-8

Library of Congress Cataloging-in-Publication Data

Names: Davis, Stephen, 1948- author.
Title: A long and bloody task : the Atlanta Campaign from
Dalton through
Kennesaw to the Chattahoochee, May 5-July 18, 1864 / by
Stephen Davis.
Description: First edition. | El Dorado Hills, California : Savas
Beatie LLC,
2016. | Series: Emerging Civil War series
Identifiers: LCCN 2016010815| ISBN 9781611213171 (pbk :
alk. paper) | ISBN
9781611213188 (ebk.)
Subjects: LCSH: Atlanta Campaign, 1864.
Classification: LCC E476.7 .D39 2016 | DDC 973.7/36--dc23
LC record available at http://lccn.loc.gov/2016010815

Published by
Savas Beatie LLC
989 Governor Drive, Suite 102
El Dorado Hills, California 95762
Phone: 916-941-6896
Email: sales@savasbeatie.com
Web: www.savasbeatie.com

Savas Beatie titles are available at special discounts for bulk purchases
in the United States by corporations, institutions, and other
organizations. For more details, please contact Special Sales, P.O.
Box 4527, El Dorado Hills, CA 95762, or you may e-mail us as at
sales@savasbeatie.com, or visit our website at www.savasbeatie.com for
additional information.

Pro mea dulce sed septentrionale uxore

Table of Contents

List of Maps

Maps by Hal Jespersen

Acknowledgments

When writing a book, an author leans on a lot of his friends and colleagues in the Civil War community. We may be a beleaguered lot in the national conversation about race and politics, so when we stick together to advance our cause—that of learning about the nation's most momentous event, our civil war—it's not just reassuring, but rejuvenating.

For this title of the Emerging Civil War Series, I wish to thank Chris Mackowski and Daniel Davis for their invitation to write about the Atlanta campaign. We signed the deal during the 2015 U.S. Memorial Day weekend activities at Kennesaw Mountain National Battlefield Park, among Yankee and Rebel reenactors (talk about rejuvenation!), which made the event that much more memorable.

I thank my friends who have written Appendices for this title: Britt McCarley, Steven Briggs, and Mike Shaffer. Their knowledge of, respectively, Sherman's logistics, Pickett's Mill battlefield, and Johnston's Chattahoochee River line is, in my view, unmatched among today's Civil War scholars. Having them share this with readers of our book is a special honor. Thanks, too, to Robert "Bobby" Novak for sharing his personal reminiscences about Kennesaw Mountain. The future of Civil War scholarship is in very good hands.

As in all my Civil War endeavors, my thanks go to Dr. Gordon Jones, senior military historian of the Atlanta History Center. In our regular barbecue luncheons, Gordon and I share military lore, tackle factual questions in the literature, and generally slay the enemy—commonly defined by us as *what we still don't know about the war.* It's great to have such friends.

Most of all, I express my sincerest gratitude to Theodore P. Savas, esq. Ted, founder of Savas Woodbury several decades ago, who gave me one of my first big chances to write about the Atlanta campaign. Now, I might say that writing this volume for Savas Beatie brings my scholarship on the subject to full circle

—except for the fact that this wouldn't be true. Ted understands as well as any Civil War publisher in the business that we are still, and always, finding new stuff about our common passion. It's this *gaudium eruditionis*—joy of knowledge—which keeps all of us Civil Warriors (to quote Bob Dylan) forever young.

Thanks to you all. Now, let's get back to the Yanks and the Rebs. . . .

Stephen Davis
Atlanta
March 2016

Photo Credits:
Dan Davis (dd); Steve Davis (sd); Library of Congress (loc); Chris Mackowski (cm); Britt McCarley (bm); Robert Novak (rn); Dave Powell (dp); Savas Beatie (sb); Michael Shaffer (ms); Wikipedia (w)

For the Emerging Civil War Series

Theodore P. Savas, *publisher*
Chris Mackowski, *series editor*
Kristopher D. White, *chief historian*
Sarah Keeney, *editorial consultant*

Maps by Hal Jespersen
Historical content editing by Daniel T. Davis
Art direction by Daniel T. Davis
Design and layout by H.R. Gordon
Publication supervision by Chris Mackowski

"The approach of warm weather told us that our work for the summer would soon commence, but I do not think anyone had a thought that the task would prove so long and bloody."

— *diary of Sgt. James Litton Cooper, 20th Tennessee, spring 1864*

Gen. Joe Johnston Defends Richmond

PROLOGUE

MAY 1862

In the spring of 1862 Gen. Joseph E. Johnston was in charge of Confederate forces in Virginia. Opposing him was Maj. Gen. George B. McClellan, whose Army of the Potomac numbered some 100,000 men. McClellan's goal, under orders from President Lincoln, was to capture the Confederate capital, Richmond. Johnston's job, under orders from President Jefferson Davis, was to defend it.

In mid-March, McClellan began moving his huge army from Washington to the peninsula of southeastern Virginia, intending to march up the James and York rivers toward the Confederate capital. Johnston developed his campaign plan and on April 14 explained it to President Davis' military advisor, Gen. Robert E. Lee. It was to bring reinforcements from the Valley, concentrate in front of Richmond, and fight a pitched battle when McClellan was as far away from his supply base as possible.

Lee argued against the plan, stressing that the enemy should be held as long as possible on the lower Peninsula. There a small Confederate force at Yorktown watched the Yankees build up their forces. The president sided with Lee.

So ordered, Johnston held his Yorktown lines another three weeks, aided immensely by McClellan's commitment to a formal siege and preparation for a huge artillery bombardment. During this period, in late April, Johnston reminded Lee repeatedly of his intent to fall back on Richmond. Hints of pessimism, even defeatism, tinged these messages, as on April 29 when Johnston warned that McClellan's impending barrage would begin a fight "which we cannot win.

The battle of Seven Pines, fought outside of Richmond, May 30-31, 1862, ended Gen. Joseph E. Johnston's tenure as commander of the Confederate Army of Northern Virginia. He would never get it back from Gen. Robert E. Lee. (dd)

Though vastly outnumbered, Southern forces held their position at Yorktown until early May 1862. (loc)

The result is certain; the time only doubtful." Worse, if the Yankees used their naval strength to advance up the James River, "the fall of Richmond would be inevitable, unless we anticipated it." With McClellan's siege artillery about to open fire at Yorktown, in the first week of May Johnston planned his withdrawal. As he did so, his message to the president on May 1 was anything but inspiring: "we can do nothing here....The enemy will give us no chance to win. We must lose. By delay we may insure the loss of Richmond too."

Johnston evacuated his lines at Yorktown, May 3-4. As he had announced to Lee and Davis, he moved his army as fast as he could up the Peninsula toward Richmond, fearing the Federals' use of river transport to lodge troops on his flank. By May 9 Johnston had taken his army to a line 20 miles of the capital. McClellan and his 100,000 men were marching slowly but inexorably up the York and Pamunkey Rivers toward Richmond. Justifiably concerned, President Davis and General Lee visited Johnston at his headquarters on the 12th to hear what he planned to do. Johnston, though, gave them nothing more specific than his intent to await McClellan's approach

LEFT: Maj. Gen. George B. McClellan, "the Young Napoleon," commander of the Federal Army of the Potomac. (loc)

RIGHT: Gen. Joseph E. Johnston, commanding Confederate forces in Virginia, began hinting pessimistically of the fall of Richmond even before McClellan's army approached the capital. (loc)

and look for an opportunity to give battle.

On May 15, Johnston ordered his forces back across the Chickahominy. In the next several days they moved almost to the outskirts of Richmond. With the enemy drawing nearby, the president grew ever more anxious for knowledge of his field commander's plans. Both he and Lee wrote Johnston on the 17th. Johnston, unfortunately, chose not to reply. Only on May 18 did Davis learn that, far from contesting McClellan's crossing of the Chickahominy, Johnston had given up his line near the river and some of his troops were now camped in the virtual suburbs of the capital. Surprised and distressed, Davis rode to headquarters and asked Johnston to come into the city and explain his plans. The general instead sent two letters which did not disclose plans to defeat the enemy. Finally, on May 21, Davis again had Lee write, this time more directly. "The President desires to know…the programme of operations which you propose….I would therefore respectfully suggest that you communicate your views on this subject directly to the President." Even to this Johnston chose not to reply directly, sending a letter to Lee on May 22, which revealed nothing of how he planned to drive McClellan back.

Finally, on the 23rd, Lee learned in a meeting with Johnston that he had begun to plan an attack. McClellan had brought his army just 10 miles from Richmond, positioning it on both sides of the Chickahominy—three corps on the north bank, two on the south. This gave the Confederates, now 75,000 strong, the opportunity to assault part of the enemy army while the rest of it watched, unable to assist. Obligingly, McClellan gave Johnston all the time he needed. The Federal commander's plan was to bring up his heavy artillery, as he had prepared to do at

The battle of Fair Oaks changed the destinies of Joseph E. Johnston and Robert E. Lee—and indeed, changed the entire complexion of the war in the East and West. (loc)

Gen. Robert E. Lee in the spring of 1862 held "the thankless post of military advisor to Jefferson Davis," as historian Robert K. Krick has termed it. (loc)

Yorktown, and bombard the Rebels from siege lines.

Finally, on May 31st, Johnston attacked that part of McClellan's army on the south side of the Chickahominy, near Seven Pines. The Confederate assault achieved some initial success, but then lost momentum. Toward the end of the day shell fragments struck Johnston in his chest and thigh. The general was borne from the field on stretcher, treated, and carried into Richmond. The next afternoon Robert E. Lee arrived to take command and ordered the army back to its original positions.

Lee never gave up command of the Army of Northern Virginia. The rest is history, as we say.

But Joe Johnston had shown several aspects of his army generalship. When faced by a numerically superior enemy force, fall back to the prize city. Don't tell your superiors in Richmond what you plan to do. If you had to, keep it vague. Wait till the enemy had gotten just outside its objective, then attack and hope for the best.

It was a formula that Johnston would use again two years later in the Atlanta campaign.

Joe Johnston never seemed to meet a defensible river that he didn't like to give up. In 1862 outside Richmond, it was the Chickahominy. He would repeat the practice in Georgia in 1864 along the Etowah. (dd)

The War in the Spring of 1864

CHAPTER ONE

MAY 1864

In early May of 1864, the main Union army in Virginia, Maj. Gen. George G. Meade's Army of the Potomac, sat in the very same locale it had been a year before: in central Virginia, about to cross the Rappahannock River to advance against Confederate Gen. Robert E. Lee's Army of Northern Virginia.

Across the Appalachian Mountains—what both sides in the American Civil War called "the west"—Union forces were in a far better position than they had been the year before. They had taken Tennessee's last two major cities, Knoxville and Chattanooga. In doing so, they had cut one of the South's most important railroad lines, that connecting the western Confederacy directly with Richmond *via* Knoxville and the Cumberland Gap.

More significantly, Maj. Gen. George H. Thomas' Army of the Cumberland had attacked and defeated Gen. Braxton Bragg's Army of Tennessee outside of Chattanooga and had driven it from the field in the war's first rout of a major Confederate army. The fleeing Southerners left behind 47 cannon—the worst battlefield loss of artillery by either side up to that point in the war.

In short, the United States government's war to conquer Southerners rebelling against its authority, and to forcibly bring its seceded states back into the Union, was in the spring of 1864 stalemated in the east, but being won in the west.

For this reason, Abraham Lincoln, president of

With Union capture of Confederate strongholds at Vicksburg and Port Hudson, the Mississippi River, "Father of Waters," fell under Union control in July 1863. (dd)

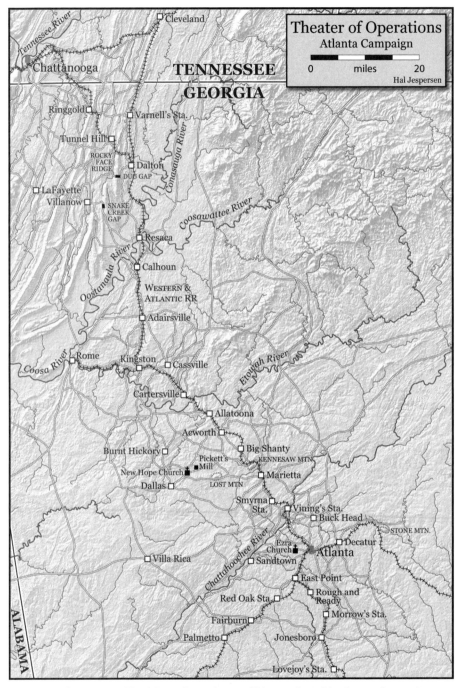

Theater of Operations
Atlanta Campaign

0   miles   20
Hal Jespersen

THEATER OF OPERATIONS—The Atlanta Campaign would be conducted by the warring armies over the 80 miles of north Georgia between Dalton and Atlanta.

In June 1862 Gen. Braxton Bragg took charge of what would be named the Army of Tennessee after Pres. Davis removed Gen. P. G. T. Beauregard from its command. (loc)

Maj. Gen. George H. Thomas earned his nickname, "the Rock of Chickamauga," with his defensive stand on the second day of the battle in September 1863. (loc)

In early 1864 Maj. Gen. Ulysses S. Grant was brought east, promoted to lieutenant general, and named general-in-chief of Union armies. (loc)

those "United" States, had decided to bring his most successful general, Maj. Gen. Ulysses S. Grant, from Tennessee to Virginia. Grant had given the North its first important victory of the war, the capture of Forts Henry and Donelson. Two months later, Grant had beaten the Rebels in the big battle at Shiloh, east of Memphis. In March 1864, in a White House ceremony, Lincoln presented Grant with his commission as lieutenant general. Only George Washington had held that rank in the U. S. Army. More importantly, Lincoln made Grant general-in-chief of all Federal forces, with authority to form and direct strategy in every theater of the war. Because whipping Lee's tough Rebel army and capturing the Confederate capital at Richmond were the North's chief priorities, Grant would take his place in the field with Meade's army, directing its coming offensive.

Who would take Grant's place in the west? When he boarded his train to Washington, Grant was commander of the "Military Division of the Mississippi," encompassing the whole area between the Appalachians and the Mississippi River. To succeed him in this position he could have recommended Maj. Gen. George H. Thomas, but Grant preferred another officer who had fought under him at Shiloh and in the Vicksburg Campaign, Maj. Gen. William Tecumseh Sherman.

Sherman was a West Pointer, class of 1840, but had not served in the Mexican War. Disillusioned with his military career, he resigned from the army in 1853. Over the next few years he worked several jobs, including as a banker in California, and failed in all of them. He quit his job as superintendent of a Louisiana military academy when that state seceded in January 1861. When war broke out, he secured a Union colonelcy and eventually promotion to brigadier. He saw action at Manassas, then was transferred to Kentucky to help organize the Union forces there.

A fellow officer once characterized "Cump" Sherman as "a splendid piece of machinery with all of the screws a little loose." When Sherman called for 200,000 troops to launch an offensive into Tennessee, the press started calling him "insane." The War Department sent him home in November 1861 to recover from what was likely a mental breakdown.

Sherman returned to service a few months later in forces commanded by Grant. The two men's friendship grew despite Sherman's spotty performance as a battlefield commander at Shiloh (April 1862), Chickasaw Bluffs (December 1862), and Missionary Ridge (November 1863). It was to Sherman that Grant handed over command of the Military Division on March 18, 1864.

The two generals soon met in Cincinnati to discuss Grant's plan for the coming spring campaign: a simultaneous advance by all Union armies. Lincoln had called for this in January 1862, and had largely been derided for it. Now, two years further into a bloody war, Grant was determined to bring the North's superior manpower and logistical resources to bear against the rebellion and to crush it. When Grant with Meade's army moved against Lee in Virginia, other Union armies were also to advance. Grant wanted Maj. Gen. Nathaniel Banks, for example, to lead a force against Mobile. Sherman would set out from Chattanooga against the Rebel army in north Georgia, the Army of Tennessee.

Confederate General Joseph E. Johnston commanded that Confederate army. At the start of the war Johnston, a West Pointer and career army officer, had risen to the rank of brigadier general when he resigned to follow his native Virginia into the

Confederacy. Quickly named C. S. brigadier, Johnston was assigned commands in the Shenandoah Valley and in northern Virginia where, with Brig. Gen. G. T. Beauregard, he helped orchestrate the Confederates' victory at Manassas in July 1861. Taking command of the Southern army in Virginia, he faced the Union advance against

Richmond in spring of 1862. After Federal Maj. Gen. George B. McClellan began marching his huge Army of the Potomac up Virginia's peninsula between the York and James rivers, Johnston assembled his forces there, but gradually retreated back toward the capital. Finally, in late May, virtually ordered by Confederate president Jefferson Davis and his military advisor Robert E. Lee to attack McClellan, Johnston did so. In the resulting battle of Seven Pines, he was seriously wounded on May 31. The next day, Lee took command of Johnston's army and never relinquished it for the rest of the war.

Shiloh Methodist meeting house stood 2.5 miles southwest of the Tennessee River landing. The small log building survived the battle of April 1862, but not the war. This is a reconstruction. (dd)

Johnston convalesced and reported for duty to the secretary of war in November 1862. There was no army-level command position open at the time, so the Davis administration created a big super-department from the Appalachians to the Mississippi and placed Johnston in charge of it. In his territory were three Confederate armies: Gen. Braxton Bragg's in middle Tennessee; Lt. Gen. John C. Pemberton's in Mississippi; and Lt. Gen. E. Kirby Smith's in east Tennessee. Unfortunately, Johnston's authority over them was vague; as a result, he did little, even when Grant in May 1863 began marching against Pemberton at Vicksburg. The administration threw together a makeshift relief army of some 20,000 and urged Johnston to attack Grant as he besieged Pemberton. Johnston moved too little and too late; Pemberton surrendered July 4. President Davis later said that Vicksburg fell for "want of provisions inside, and a general outside who wouldn't fight."

Lt. Gen. William J. Hardee has the distinction of being the longest-serving corps commander in the Amy of Tennessee. (loc)

Maj. Gen. William T. Sherman never tired of lecturing his troops on the "proper method" of wrecking railroads, especially heating and twisting the iron rails so they could not be used unless reforged. Here is one of "Sherman's neckties," seen on Meridian's Civil War trail. (dd)

Nevertheless, when an army-level command position developed later that year, Davis gave it to Joseph E. Johnston. After the ignominious rout of his army at Missionary Ridge in November 1863, Braxton Bragg resigned; senior corps command Lt. Gen. William J. Hardee took temporary charge. Two weeks later, Johnston was named commander of the Army of Tennessee. He assumed his responsibilities on December 27 at Dalton, Georgia.

During the next several months the new commander worked at building up the troops' spirits, like issuing furloughs; increasing the food, clothing and supplies brought by train from Atlanta; and instituting procedures to shore up discipline in the ranks. Previously the Army of Tennessee's infantry, divided into two corps, was commanded by Lieutenant Gen. Hardee and Maj. Gen. Thomas C. Hindman, who took over Maj. Gen. John C. Breckinridge's corps when the latter left for Virginia. Hardee was experienced and reliable, and with Johnston's arrival at Dalton he reverted to corps commander without complaining. He would stay. Hindman's appointment, however, was temporary. Johnston wanted someone else to command his second corps. When he heard that John Bell Hood, famed division commander in Lee's army, had recovered from his wound at Chickamauga and had been promoted to lieutenant general, Johnston asked that Hood be sent to his army. The War Department complied.

By that time, Maj. Gen. William T. Sherman, commanding the Army of the Tennessee, had led 26,000 Northern soldiers across the width of Mississippi, from Vicksburg to Meridian, in a raid whose sole purpose was to tear up Southern railroads, burn factories and shops, and destroy every other form of property that could be deemed of "military value." Sherman intended his men to live "off the country"; he had learned it could be done from Grant the year before in the march on Vicksburg.

Opposing Sherman was Lt. Gen. Leonidas Polk, whom President Davis had shipped off from Bragg's army after Chickamauga (Bragg actually asked that Polk be courtmartialed for insubordination in the battle). Polk was given command of the Army of Mississippi, which had been assembled for Johnston to use against Grant at Vicksburg (but which he did not). Polk had only 10,000 infantry and as many scattered cavalry. He pleaded for reinforcements.

On February 18, after Sherman's raiding column reached Meridian, an alarmed Jefferson Davis ordered Johnston at Dalton to send Hardee's corps off toward Montgomery to aid Polk. Hardee's troops boarded the trains for Atlanta and beyond; on February 22, Maj. Gen. Benjamin Franklin Cheatham's division reached Montgomery. By then, however, having burned much of Meridian, Sherman's troops were marching back toward Vicksburg, doing more damage to government (and civilian) property. Hardee's infantry eventually returned to Johnston's army.

The brilliant, eccentric Maj. Gen. William T. Sherman, was once called "a splendid piece of machinery with all of the screws a little loose." (loc)

So Sherman, who boasted of his army's destruction of Meridian, was acting offensively, in both senses of the term. The Confederate government also wanted Joe Johnston to show some offense. Even before he took command of the army, Davis wrote him suggesting that after refitting his troops he develop a plan for advancing back into Tennessee.

This was only the first such message from Davis, Seddon and Bragg, who in late February was appointed military advisor to the president. The correspondence was carried on for several months, with Johnston repeating that he was outnumbered by the enemy, that they were well fortified in Chattanooga, and that he lacked both subsistence and transport to get around them in a forward movement.

Johnston was actually correct; the government was asking too much of him. But to Jefferson Davis, who recalled Johnston's retreat up the Peninsula and his dithering in Mississippi, the whole episode again indicated that the general commanding the South's second-largest army lacked a fighting spirit.

JOSEPH E. JOHNSTON
1807 — 1891
BRIGADIER GENERAL U.S.A.
GENERAL C.S.A.
GIVEN COMMAND OF THE CONFEDERATE
FORCES AT DALTON IN
1863. HE DIRECTED THE 79 DAYS
CAMPAIGN TO ATLANTA, ONE OF THE
MOST MEMORABLE IN THE ANNALS OF WAR
ERECTED BY BRYAN M. THOMAS
CHAPTER UNITED DAUGHTERS OF
CONFEDERACY, DALTON, GEORGIA, 1912

Sherman Launches His Campaign

CHAPTER TWO

MAY 5-9, 1864

Sherman broke the Confederates' deadlock by launching his own spring campaign, which immediately put Johnston and his army on the defensive.

Before he did so, Sherman and Grant exchanged letters in which they repeated their understanding of the goals of the coming offensive. "You I propose to move against Johnston's army," Grant wrote on April 4, "to break it up and to get into the interior of the enemy's country as far as you can, inflicting all the damage you can against their War resources."

Sherman answered promptly on the 10th: "I will not let side issues draw me off from your main plan in which I am to knock Joe Johnston, and do as much damage to the resources of the enemy as possible."

Sherman's reply is important for two reasons. First, neither general mentioned anything about Atlanta, only getting into "the enemy's country"; but it was obvious that Federal forces marching south from Chattanooga would be headed for Atlanta. Second, notice the difference between Grant's hope that his friend Cump would *break up* Johnston's army, and Sherman's promise that he would merely *knock* it. Sherman's subtle change in his understanding of Grant's orders underscores an aspect of his generalship that he had already demonstrated thus far in the war: that he was a mediocre (at best) battle captain, and that he tended to avoid big, bloody and

They loved Joe Johnston in Dalton. This statue, dedicated in 1912, was erected by the local chapter of the United Daughters of the Confederacy. Note the inscription that he "directed" the campaign (not Sherman), and that his campaign of retreating to Atlanta was "one of the most memorable in the annals of war." (dd)

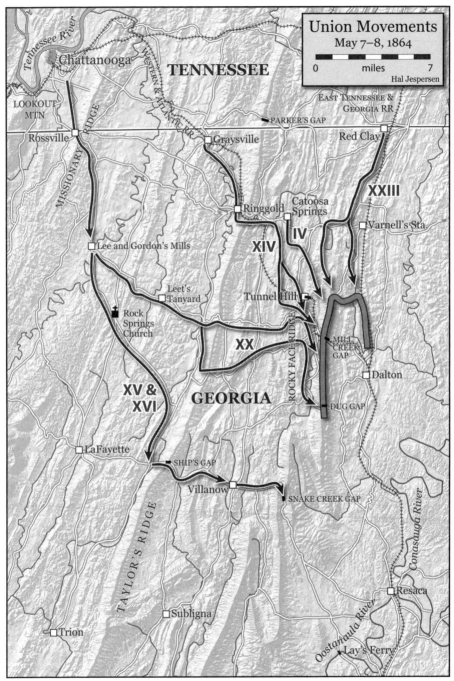

UNION MOVEMENTS—Just as Grant wanted, Sherman got his army group moving May 5, 1864, the day Grant advanced against Lee in the Wilderness.

potentially campaign-ending battles. ("Of course I must fight when the time comes," he had written a daughter in January 1864. "But wherever a result can be accomplished without Battle I prefer it.")

Sherman's real strength lay in maneuver. He had the extra advantage of a formidable numerical superiority over Joe Johnston's army. Available to him was not just George Thomas' Army of the Cumberland near Chattanooga, but Maj. Gen. James B. McPherson's Army of the Tennessee then in north Alabama (which had been under Sherman until his elevation to military division command), as well as Maj. Gen. John M. Schofield's Army of the Ohio, which had been operating in east Tennessee. Once these forces were assembled, Sherman was confident that he could force Johnston to give up the territory of north Georgia, all the way back to Atlanta.

Sherman wrote Grant that he had met with his senior officers "and have signified only to . . . Schofield, Thomas and McPherson our general plans." He did not elaborate how he would use his three armies in those "general plans," but it is likely that to his three army commanders he would have outlined his idea of using Thomas' army to fix the Rebels in place with sorties, skirmishing and shelling, while using McPherson's smaller army or perhaps Schofield's to march and maneuver around Johnston's flank, compelling him to retreat lest he be cut off from his line of supply. Again, Sherman did not give Grant details but as we shall see, throughout the Georgia Campaign Sherman would repeatedly outflank Johnston by sending McPherson or Schofield from his right in a flanking march around the Rebel left.

Now here is the important prediction he made to Grant on April 10: "should Johnston fall behind the Chattahoochee I would feign to the right, but pass to the left, and act on Atlanta or on its eastern communications, according to developed facts." With this statement, Sherman was signaling that throughout the campaign he would outflank Johnston by sending columns from the Federal right, but once he had finally reached the Rebels at their climactic position, the Chattahoochee (their last geographic barrier), he would reverse himself: feint to the right but cross troops over the river from his left, thus forcing

Maj. Gen. John McAllister Schofield, commander of the XXIII Corps. Named the Army of the Ohio, it was the smallest of the three in Sherman's army group. The closest the Confederates came to this kind of concentration occurred in mid-May 1864, when Lt. Gen. Leonidas Polk's Army of Mississippi joined Johnston's Army of Tennessee around Resaca. Polk's forces were officially recognized as the Army of Tennessee's third infantry corps in late July '64. By then, General Polk was dead. (loc)

The view from Mill Creek Gap to Rocky Face Ridge encompassed these heights, 1,500 feet above sea level. (dd)

the enemy to retreat before Sherman's final approach to Atlanta.

It is easy to overestimate the importance of Sherman's outline of plan in his letter of April 10 to Grant, which he wrote a full three weeks before the Georgia campaign even opened. In this exaggerative vein, it is possible to imagine what might have happened if the Confederates had learned of Sherman's plan for crossing the Chattahoochee beforehand. What if the Germans had learned of Eisenhower's plan to merely feint to the left (threaten crossing the English Channel at Calais), but actually strike on the right (that is, land all of his forces on the beaches of Normandy)? This is why historical might-have-beens, especially in military history, are so intriguing—and so profitless.

But the point made here is that a month before his Georgia campaign even opened, General Sherman had a plan to use his superior numbers to force Johnston's army back through north Georgia in repeated, identical flanking maneuvers. Then, at the Chattahoochee, he planned to switch his tactics in what would be the campaign's most important coup.

What Sherman could not tell Grant was that he would refuse to implement the tactics that his superior officer would use to batter Robert E. Lee's army into submission: frontal assaults, relying upon superior numbers and repeated blows to win the Virginia Campaign, essentially by a war of attrition. Instead, as we will see, Sherman would use his superior numbers to fix Johnston's army in position while outflanking it. And superior numbers Sherman definitely had at the start of the campaign:

• Thomas' Army of the Cumberland: 61,600 infantry in the IV, XIV and XX Corps;

• McPherson's Army of the Tennessee: 22,300 infantry in the XV and XVI Corps;

• Schofield's Army of the Ohio: 9,200 infantry of the XXIII Corps;

• cavalry, mostly in Thomas' army: 12, 400;

• and artillery: 4,500 men serving 254 guns.

General Johnston did not know Sherman's exact strength—110,000 officers and men in all three armies—but, as he had repeated to Davis, Seddon and

In the 1930s, the Works Progress Administration in President Franklin D. Roosevelt's New Deal established five "pocket parks" in north Georgia, alongside U.S. Highway 41 from Tunnel Hill to New Hope. Each one has a metal plaque with map. This one, in front of the State Patrol headquarters on U.S. 41, shows how McPherson's flanking march through Snake Creek Gap forced Johnston's army to retreat back to Resaca. (dd)

These undisturbed Confederate earthworks are located near the Georgia State Patrol building on U.S. 41 northwest of Dalton. Brig. Gen. Randall Gibson's Louisiana brigade and the Eufaula (Alabama) battery occupied the fort. (dd)

Bragg, he knew he was outnumbered.

Moreover, because he knew that the government had hoped for him to adopt an offensive policy, at the start of the campaign he could not tell Richmond he planned to do just the opposite: build defensive fortifications at strong topographic positions and hope Sherman would attack him there.

By this point in the war, it had been shown time and again that veteran infantry, well dug in and armed with rifled muskets, could repulse (and bloodily) just about every enemy infantry attack thrown against them. Indeed, after Lee's rather easy victory at Fredericksburg, Johnston is said to have snidely commented: "What luck some people have. Nobody will ever come to attack me in such a place." Here, in north Georgia, he hoped to be proven wrong.

Johnston had half of Sherman's strength. Returns for the Army of Tennessee on April 30, eve of the campaign's onset, showed 42,900 infantry in Hardee's and Hood's corps, 7,800 cavalrymen and 3,100

Much of the Confederate line at Dalton ran north-south along Rocky Face Ridge, but a mile or so east of Tunnel Hill it turned perpendicularly to the east, running into Crow Valley. This sector was held by Hood's Corps. (dd)

cannoneers (with 144 guns) for a total of 53,800 men present for duty. Not counted in the army returns was the immense number of slaves—teamsters, hospital stewards, officers' servants—who performed tasks otherwise assigned to soldiers.

During the winter of 1863-64, Johnston had deployed his troops north and west of Dalton along Rocky Face Ridge. The tall ridge (800 hundred feet high in places) runs north-south for miles. Particularly because of its western "rocky face," it was an ideal defensive position for Johnston's army. The Confederates' seven-mile line ran along the Rocky Face crest, and then north of Dalton it turned east perpendicularly into Crow Valley. The ridge is perforated by two gaps.

The main one is Mill Creek Gap, also known as Buzzard Roost, northwest of Dalton. Through it ran the main road and the Western & Atlantic Railroad, the single-track line connecting Atlanta with Chattanooga. During the winter, Confederates had dammed up Mill Creek and created a lake in the gap, which would impede any Yankee infantry assault. Drawing up before the Rebel lines at the gap, Federals could see the buzzards roosting in the heights ahead of them. One asked a comrade what he thought the birds were doing up there. "Counting us," came the ominous reply.

The second pass in the ridge, Dug Gap, cuts

Save the Dalton Battlefields, LLC, is very proud of the undisturbed earthworks still to be seen in Whitfield County. Evidence is this artillery fort occupied by Confederate Capt. Max Van Den Corput's Cherokee Battery, located behind Poplar Spring Baptist Church. (dd)

In spring 1864, Alfred Waud was illustrating Grant's campaign in Virginia for *Harper's Weekly*. But after the war, visiting Georgia, he completed a number of works depicting the Atlanta campaign. This white and black ink wash painting shows Union infantry charging up Dug Gap Mountain on May 8. They were repulsed by Confederate cavalrymen holding the crest. (loc)

through it three miles south of Mill Creek. On February 25, Thomas' troops had sallied against the thin Rebel line there and almost broken through it before Johnston called in reinforcements to block the attack.

The incident caused Thomas to send probes farther south along Rocky Face looking for other gaps. Sure enough, they found one a dozen miles south of Dalton: Snake Creek Gap. It did not look as if the Southerners had yet put troops there to guard it. The discovery allowed Thomas to give Sherman his idea for flanking Johnston out of his Rocky Face line: Schofield and McPherson to demonstrate against the Rebels while Thomas' Army of the Cumberland swept around south, through Snake Creek Gap, and marched east to cut Johnston's supply line, the Western & Atlantic.

Sherman liked Thomas' plan, but altered it. For the task of marching through Snake Creek and flanking Johnston out of position, he assigned McPherson's Army of the Tennessee.

The W. & A. would be the central feature of both sides' supply operations. Completed in 1850, it ran 138 miles from Atlanta to Chattanooga. To Johnston's army in Dalton, the railroad brought supplies from Atlanta, and as Johnston retreated back toward Atlanta, he always kept close to the W. & A. The railroad's key topographical feature in north Georgia was the 1,477-foot tunnel cut through the Chetoogeta Mountain, a dozen miles northwest of Dalton. During the winter of '63-'64, Confederates never planned to blow the tunnel, as the Southern cavalryman

Brig. Gen. John H. Morgan had done at Gallatin, Tennessee, in August 1862. That feat had knocked out the Federals' use of the Nashville-Louisville railway for three months. If Johnston had similarly destroyed the Chetoogeta tunnel before he began withdrawing in the first days of the Federal advance, Sherman would have started the Georgia Campaign with a big chore—clearing the railroad tunnel—before his troops could make their first march.

The Union commander had calculated that to feed and supply his 110,000 men and 50,000 animals he needed 65 to 80 freight cars daily bringing food and freight from the army's big base at Nashville. As he advanced farther into Georgia, Sherman would take much precaution to protect his Western & Atlantic supply line.

As part of his plan for a simultaneous advance of all Union armies, Grant instructed Sherman to have his troops prepared to march forward on May 5. In the days before that, Johnston could see the activity along the enemy front. On May 1, he suggested that ladies who had been sharing quarters with their officer-husbands now depart for the rear.

Aware that Sherman had brought McPherson's army east, the administration in Richmond ordered Leonidas Polk to bring his army eastward as well to join Johnston. Polk's troops would take the train to northeast Alabama and then march *via* Rome, Georgia, to join Johnston's army at Dalton.

Polk's reinforcement would not arrive before Sherman began his advance. In its opening days, May 5-7, Thomas moved against Rocky Face from the northwest with his three corps, the IV, XIV and XX. Schofield's "army" of the XXIII Corps moved

Completion in May 1850 of the 1,477 foot-long tunnel north of Dalton allowed the Western & Atlantic Railroad to begin operating between Atlanta and Chattanooga. Confederate forces retreating from Dalton did not attempt to blow up or block the vital tunnel, which was crucial to Sherman's logistical operations for his army group. (dd)

down on the ridge from the north. While these forces skirmished with the Rebels at various points (including Dug Gap), to the south McPherson's Army of the Tennessee (the XV and XVI Corps) marched toward Snake Creek Gap and entered it on the 8th. As Thomas had predicted, the pass was only lightly defended. On May 9, McPherson's infantry brushed aside some Confederate cavalry, pushed through the cut and headed for the railroad south of Dalton.

Southern cavalry held this position along the crest of Dug Gap Mountain on May 8 when John Geary's infantry attacked to divert attention from McPherson's maneuver through Snake Creek Gap. Dug Gap Mountain Battlefield Park is owned by the Whitfield-Murry Historical Society and is free and open to the public. (dd)

Resaca

CHAPTER THREE

MAY 14-15, 1864

"Mac," as he was known to his friend Cump Sherman, had been given clear orders: "I want you to move to . . . Snake Gap, secure it and from it make a bold attack on the enemy's flank or his railroad at any point between Tilton and Resaca" (Tilton was midway between Dalton and Resaca).

As it emerged from the gap, McPherson's advance was less than six miles from Resaca, a railroad town on the W. & A. a dozen miles south of Dalton. In the hills west of Resaca was a regiment of Confederate infantry guarding the town and the nearby railroad bridge over the Oostanaula River. On May 5, Johnston had taken the precaution of sending an infantry brigade to Resaca. After his cavalry reported late on the 8th that Yankees were west of Tilton and heading south, Johnston sent a cavalry brigade to Resaca as well. Once there, it headed west toward Snake Creek Gap early on the 9th.

That morning, McPherson's infantry, attacked by the Southern horsemen, beat them back and marched farther east. By mid-afternoon the Federals had taken a bald hill just one mile west of the town. From there they could see their prize: the railroad bridge over the Oostanaula. But they could also see some 1,400 Rebels dug in at a fort on the river's north bank guarding the rail bridge.

General McPherson, soon to arrive, worried an enemy column might be marching down from Dalton to strike him in flank. But he was without cavalry to scout the enemy position or movements. So he did the

Modern view of the Resaca battlefield. Here, the area of Hood's attack (dd)

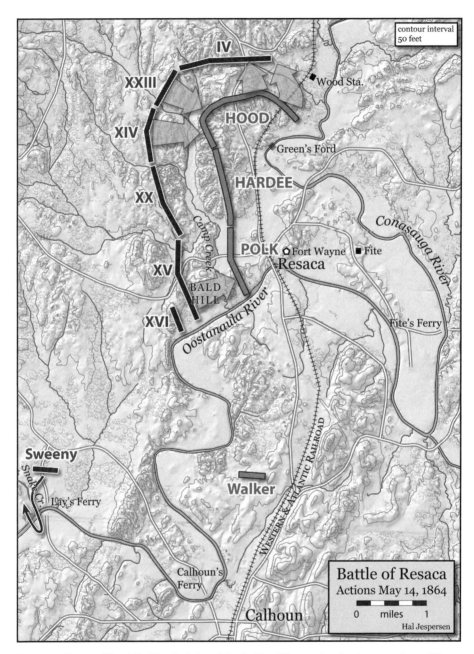

BATTLE OF RESACA (MAY 14)—The first day of the battle of Resaca involved a swapping of blows. The Confederates enjoyed temporary success in their attack against the Federal left. McPherson's assault against the Rebel left gained some high ground near the river bridges.

thing cautious commanders usually do: he ordered his troops to fall back, all the way to Snake Creek Gap.

On learning this, Sherman was furious. "Well, Mac, you have missed the opportunity of a lifetime," he admonished. To be sure, McPherson had lost his nerve: a more audacious commander would have pushed forward to Resaca, interdicted the railroad, maybe shelled or burned the bridge, and waited to see if the enemy would try to drive him off. In fairness to McPherson, this was his first action as army commander; he had only taken charge of the Army of the Tennessee when Sherman was elevated to the military division post. But Sherman was right; seldom in war does an army catch the enemy off guard, steal a march into his rear, and threaten to cut his supply line.

Johnston and his army had narrowly averted disaster. Afterward, Confederates wondered why Snake Creek Gap had been unguarded. Historians continue to wrestle with the question. Johnston's apologists point their fingers at Maj. Gen. Joseph Wheeler, the army's cavalry chief, whose troopers' job was to guard the flanks. Others have blamed Johnston himself, who had had all winter to scout the area and learn of the enemy's likely approaches. The scholarly tussle continues to this day.

Despite McPherson's timidity, Sherman, determined to push through Snake Creek Gap with more troops, told McPherson to dig in while he brought them up.

On the morning of May 11, the Confederate garrison at Resaca telegraphed that the enemy was again advancing toward them. Johnston concluded he could no longer hold his Rocky Face line and began shifting troops from Dalton to Resaca, 16 miles south by rail. The Confederates' movement continued on the 12th. That evening, Johnston took one of the last trains leaving Dalton.

By then, General Polk and his small army began to arrive at Resaca and took their place in the line that Johnston's engineers had laid out. The new position ran mostly parallel to the railroad a mile or less west of it. The two flanks rested on the Conasauga River to the right and the Oostanaula below Resaca on the left. Hood's corps held the right, Hardee the center, and Polk the left. Way to the south, five miles from Dalton, Maj. Gen. William H. T. Walker's division hovered near Calhoun, watching for any enemy maneuver in that direction.

As the Confederates dug in on May 13, Sherman

Maj. Gen. Joseph Wheeler became chief of cavalry in the Army of the Mississippi (soon to be Tennessee) in July 1862. After the war, he and his family settled in north Alabama. His is one of two statues for Alabamians in Statuary Hall in the United States Capitol in Washington, D.C. (the other is for Helen Keller). (loc)

Maj. Gen. James B. McPherson (1828-1864) took command of the Army of the Tennessee on March 26, 1864. He had thus served only seven weeks in this new role when Sherman gave him the key assignment of flanking Johnston via Snake Creek Gap. (loc)

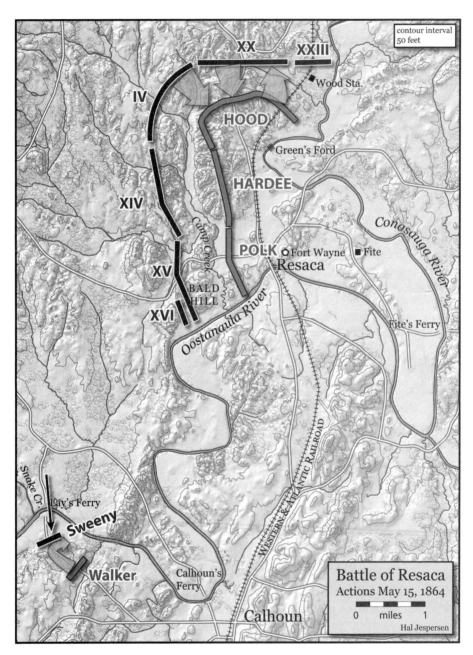

BATTLE OF RESACA (MAY 15)—On the second day of the battle, as the two sides slugged it out on the Confederate right, Union Brig. Gen. Tom Sweeny got his division across the Oostanaula. When Maj. Gen. W. H. T. Walker's division could not drive them back, Johnston had to retreat from Resaca.

brought his forces up. McPherson, through Snake Creek Gap (again), advanced on the bald hill and took it (again). The XVI Corps held the Union right, hinging on the Oostanaula. Then, as the Federal line extended northward, came the XV.

Thomas' army fell in: Maj. Gen. Joseph Hooker's XX Corps, then Maj. Gen. John Palmer's XIV. Schofield took position farther to the left. When Thomas' other corps, Maj. Gen. Oliver O. Howard's IV, came up it went in as the left flank of Sherman's line. It did not, however, extend eastward far enough to reach the Conasauga.

Johnston, entrenched at Resaca, expected Sherman to give him battle there, and Cump determined to oblige him. The two-day resulting engagement boiled down to a swapping of blows: on the first day, a Federal attack on the Confederate center-right; then a Confederate assault on the Federal left, followed by a Federal advance on the Confederate left. On the second day, May 15, the Federals launched an attack on the Confederate right, followed by a Confederate counterattack on the Federal left. In all cases, the defenders repulsed the attackers.

Brig. Gen. Absalom Baird, division commander in the XIV Corps. One of his brigade leaders described the Resaca battlefield terrain: "the face of the country was very rough, rising and falling in a succession of high hills and deep gorges, covered with an almost impenetrably dense growth of timber, rendering it a very difficult matter for troops to advance in line." (loc)

"Sherman's Department—Engagement at Snake Creek Gap, Georgia. From a Sketch by Theodore R. Davis." *Harper's Weekly* was probably the leading illustrated newspaper in the country at the start of the Civil War. Harper's and *Frank Leslie's Illustrated Newspaper* employed professional illustrators to accompany Union armies, draw pictures from the field, and mail them back to New York. There the drawings were rendered into woodcuts for printing in the papers. This image appeared in the Harper's issue of June 4, 1864. (loc)

Yet through all of this bloodletting, Sherman kept his eye far beyond his right flank. As he had attempted at Dalton, he hoped to turn Johnston's left flank: sending an infantry division well down the Oostanaula, crossing it by pontoon bridge at a place called Lay's Ferry (four miles down from the bald hill), and having it march, as McPherson had been ordered, eastward to strike the Rebel railroad south of Resaca. If the flanking column—Brigade Gen. Thomas Sweeny's division of the XVI Corps—crossed the Oostanaula and merely threatened the railroad, Sherman expected Johnston to retreat.

But note that Sherman's planned pugilism along his main line at Resaca—the several attacks he ordered, May 14-15—did not approximate in strength or determination the kind of infantry assaults being ordered by Lt. Gen. Grant about the same time, 500 miles away in Virginia. There, at Spotsylvania Courthouse on May 12, nearly 19,000 Federals massed in a huge sledge-hammer formation for a predawn attack that would thoroughly break Lee's line. Sherman had no mind for that kind of tactic; thus the infantry

South of Resaca is one of five historical pavilions built by the Federal government in the 1930s. The metal map shows the opposing armies' positions, May 13-15, and how Sweeny's flanking maneuver brought about Confederate withdrawal, "with Federals following deeper into the heart of the South." (dd)

Tourists to the Resaca battlefield area will be treated to the numerous state historical markers drafted by Atlantan Wilbur G. Kurtz (1882-1967). In the 1950s, Kurtz not only wrote the texts for these roadside markers, but told the state where he wanted them put. (dd)

advances he called for against Johnston's position should really be called reconnaissances-in-force.

The first such demonstration began around 11 a.m. on May 14 after some morning skirmishing. For four hours soldiers of four divisions belonging to the XIV and XXIII Corps charged the center-right of the enemy line. But they faced several obstacles. The Federals had had no opportunity to reconnoiter the

In Virginia, Maj. Gen. Joseph Hooker had risen from corps commander in the Army of the Potomac to leadership of the army, only to be humiliated at Chancellorsville. Hooker was sent west in October 1863 to join the Union forces at Chattanooga. At the start of the Atlanta campaign, he commanded the XX Corps. (loc)

Pennsylvanian John W. Geary commanded the 2nd Division, XX Corps, during the Atlanta campaign. Earlier, his son Eddie had served in a battery attached to his division. "Tell him to be manly, brave and true, to cast away boyishness," Geary wrote his wife Mary in June 1863 regarding another son about to enter the service. Four months later, Eddie was killed in battle near Chattanooga. He was 18 years old. (loc)

West Pointer Oliver Otis Howard, promoted to brigadier general in September 1861, lost his right arm at Seven Pines. At Chancellorsville, he led the luckless XI Corps, which was routed by Stonewall Jackson's famous flank attack. During the Atlanta campaign, he was placed in command of the Army of the Tennessee. Sherman is said to have remarked that he was pleased to put the army in the hands of General Howard. (loc)

Rebel position, and thus had no idea of its strength, which was considerable—the Confederates had been entrenching for at least a day. Hills and gorges undulated enough to tire out the attackers, who also had to trudge through thick woods and underbrush. Then there was Camp Creek, which flowed across their assault-front. "A deep, narrow stream, with quicksand in places, and steep muddy banks," one Northern officer called it. "A bog and creek into which they plunged more than waist deep," complained another.

Wallowing in the "creek," the Federals came under shellfire and musketry such that many did not try to climb up the muddy slope, but huddled under it. "Many stuck under the miry banks of the stream," reported Brig. Gen. Absalom Baird, whose division took part in the advance. Those who clambered out of the bog faced a fierce fire charging up the slope. For the Confederates dug in along the crest, repulsing the Yankee attack was "a veritable picnic," remembered a Kentuckian in Maj. Gen. William B. Bate's division, "protected as we were by earthworks, with clear and

After you've seen the earthwork embrasures for Van Den Corput's Cherokee Battery at Dalton and Resaca, a visit to Atlanta's Oakland Cemetery brings you to the captain's grave. *Requiescat in pace.* (dd)

open ground in front." Those Federals not cut down took shelter in the woods and ravines, delivering skirmish fire until darkness allowed them to retreat back across Camp Creek and to their lines.

The first Federal attack at Resaca petered out around 3 o'clock. Northern losses reached 1,600. Before the day was over, Thomas and Schofield ordered their artillery to shell the Rebel line, which caused considerable casualties among the Southerners. By the end of the day, those divisions taking part in this part of the battle—Maj. Gens. Patrick R. Cleburne's, Bate's and Thomas C. Hindman's—suffered probably 400 to 500 men lost. Included among them was Brig. Gen. William F. Tucker, so severely struck by a shell that he was literally knocked out of the war.

Then Johnston saw a chance for a punch of his own. Cavalry had brought intelligence that the enemy line did not reach the Conasauga—but Hood's did. Opportunity was thus presented for a flank attack, which Johnston ordered at 4 p.m. but which did not begin till an hour later. One soldier of Maj. Gen. David Stanley's IV Corps division, which held the far Union left, observed that the Rebels "formed in admirable order, their flags floating gaily, many of their officers mounted."

Hood's lines so overlapped Stanley's flank that the rightmost Confederate division, Maj. Gen. Peter

Maj. Gen. Carter L. Stevenson's division assaulted the Federal left on the afternoon of May 14. The Confederates initially drove the Federals back, but were eventually repulsed with help from Capt. Peter Simonson's 5th Indiana Battery. (dd)

Joe Johnston claimed in his 1874 memoir that Van Den Corput's Cherokee Battery—four Napoleon guns abandoned at Resaca—was the only material loss he incurred in the Atlanta campaign. The battery earthworks remain today on private property. The landowners graciously allow respectful visitors, but please don't park in the driveway! (dd)

Stewart's, never even encountered enemy resistance in its advance close to the river. That meant the other participating division, Maj. Gen. Carter Stevenson's, carried out the heavy work of the assault. Because Stanley's flank was indeed "in the air," Stevenson's troops were able to overlap it such that the Yankees on the extreme left actually took fire from three directions before falling back "in great disorder," as one Union officer admitted.

When the Southerners pressed their assault into an open field, they came under heavy artillery fire. The Union gunners' infantry support ran away, but they continued firing until reinforcements came up to help them hold the line and eventually drive the Rebels from the field. Stevenson's division sustained a loss of 575 in its relatively brief afternoon assault.

Generals Hood and Johnston watched the attack. While it had failed, Johnston saw its initial success and such future potential with Stewart's readjustment and participation that he ordered it renewed the next morning.

About the time Johnston ordered Hood's enveloping attack—4 o'clock—at the other end of the Federal line General McPherson ordered a frontal one. He had observed across Camp Creek some high ground that, if taken, would allow his artillery to get closer to firing on the railroad bridge across the Oostanaula. Two divisions crossed the creek on a bridge and footlogs, stormed the high ground and rousted the outnumbered Rebels.

The day was late, but General Polk recognized the threat posed by the enemy's newly taken position. At 7:30, he sent forth three brigades to retake it, but the Federals had dug in and brought up artillery. The Southerners were repulsed, and McPherson's men held their position.

The really important events that day occurred farther downstream, when Sweeny's division sought a crossing-point below the Rebel left flank. At the planned site, Lay's Ferry, the Federals found the enemy in force on the south bank. So they passed farther down still. At a point where Snake Creek empties into the Oostanaula, they crossed over on pontoon boats and drove off a Rebel detachment. But fretful that he might be counterattacked, Sweeny called his bridgehead back. Sherman showed no displeasure at this McPhersonesque forth-and-back; he was satisfied with the day's gains.

That night, word reached Johnston's headquarters that the Federals beyond his left had crossed the

More than 450 Southern soldiers are buried in Resaca's Confederate Cemetery. It was dedicated in October 1866. Local resident Mary Green led the movement to secure the land and reinter the dead buried on the nearby battlefield. (dd)

The civilian photographer George Barnard traveled with Sherman's army in its march from Atlanta to Savannah late in 1864. In the spring of 1866, he returned to Georgia, taking pictures of war scenes he intended to produce in a big album, Photographic Views of Sherman's Campaign, which was released in the fall of '66. He took a number of views of the Resaca battlefield. This one looks east from the center of the Union line In Camp Creek valley toward Confederate works beyond. Note the Federal soldiers' graves in the foreground. (loc)

Oostanaula. He responded by cancelling Hood's morning attack and sending Walker's division off in a night march toward Lay's Ferry. Early the next morning Walker sent back word that he saw no enemy on the south bank.

This meant that Sherman held the initiative on the morning of May 15, and he used it. He ordered Schofield's two divisions to the far left so the Federal line could anchor on the Conasauga. Hooker and Howard were to attack the Rebel right. And McPherson with Sweeny's division would again try to make "a good lodgment on the other bank."

At 8 a.m. Sweeny's troops recrossed the river and chased off a few Rebels on the south bank. Pontoons were laid and a bridge built, allowing an infantry brigade to march over by noon. Walker reported to HQ that the enemy was across the river and that a counterattack he ordered at Lay's Ferry had failed to drive them back.

The assault on the Confederate line ordered by Sherman began around noon, falling on Stevenson's and Hindman's divisions. The Southerners repulsed it at all points, but the Federals achieved at least one success. During the morning, General Hood had directed Stevenson to place a battery to fire at some annoying enemy artillery across the way. To hit the target, the battery had to be advanced actually 20 yards in front of the main line. Before connecting trenches could be dug, the Yankees attacked. Colonel Benjamin Harrison's 70th Indiana overwhelmed the battery, bayonetting the gunners. But Confederate musketry drove them back, so that at 3 o'clock the four Napoleon guns—belonging to Capt. Maximilien Van Den Corput's "Cherokee Battery"—stood out in the middle of no-man's-land. Southerners called out, "Come on—take those guns!" "Come on and take 'em yourselves," the Yankees yelled back.

Midafternoon, Johnston changed his mind. News from Hood that his troops had repulsed the enemy attack and Walker's morning report caused him to return to the original plan of repeating the flank attack on the Union left, which the afternoon before had come close to success. He issued orders for it, which Hood forwarded to his three division commanders.

Soon, however, Walker's later report that he had failed in his counterattack on the enemy bridgehead forced Johnston to change his mind again and cancel the afternoon assault.

The counter-order did not reach Stewart in time. At 5 p.m. his infantry advanced in a double battle-line. This time, though, Stewart's troops definitely did encounter the enemy. General Hooker had strengthened his line and braced it with artillery. The Confederates could see the enemy line on the high ground ahead of them. "Notwithstanding the almost utter impossibility of our success, apparent to everyone," remembered Capt. George W. Welch of the 38th Alabama, "the order was promptly obeyed."

The Confederates advanced a few hundred yards, driving back the Yankee skirmishers, but came under such intense fire that they gave way in 20 minutes, returning to their lines. The firing was through by 6:30.

Hood put the best face he could on the repulse, which probably cost 600-800 casualties: "General Stewart moved forward from the right with his division, driving the enemy before him, but was subsequently forced to resume his original position before largely superior numbers."

After the fighting ended on the 15th, Johnston, conferring with senior officers, decided the enemy lodgment downstream and the menacing closeness of McPherson's cannon to the main river bridges compelled his army's retreat. He issued orders, and the corps commanders planned their troops' passage that night across the train and wagon bridges, plus two pontoon spans the engineers had laid above them.

Johnston's army conducted its nighttime retreat without major hitch. Southern pickets were drawn in between 1 and 3 a.m. By 3:30, all infantry, wagons and artillery were across.

All artillery, that is, except Van Den Corput's

four lonely guns, which had to be abandoned in their embrasure in Stevenson's front. Unknown to the Southerners, in the darkness Brig. Gen. John W. Geary sent forth a detail to sneak up to the battery, dig a way of egress, tie ropes and quietly drag the guns back to the Northern lines. The Yankees succeeded in their task mainly because as they toiled in the dark, Stevenson's pickets were not about to start a firefight as their army was retreating.

After the war, when Hood and Johnston were arguing about who was right on certain points of the campaign, the Cherokee Battery came up. Johnston charged that the four guns "exposed and abandoned at Resaca by General Hood" were the only ones lost during his tenure in the campaign. Hood countered that "they were four old iron pieces, not worth the sacrifice of the life of even one man." Captain Van Den Corput's take on the squabble is not recorded.

Judging from the Confederate reports we have, Johnston's effort to hold off Sherman's advance at Resaca, and the latter's use of sortie and maneuver to get around it, cost the Army of Tennessee almost 3,000 killed, wounded, and missing. Sherman's casualties were higher, as the Federals had done more of the attacking. The wounded in all three of his armies, he reported, totaled 3,375. The number of dead was not yet in by the 16th, but he figured that it "will not exceed the usual proportion." That proportion, in the Civil War, was usually one soldier dead to another five wounded. That would mean about 600 Federals slain, and a U.S. casualty toll at Resaca of about 4,000. (Grant's losses at Spotsylvania, May 10-12, were twice that, further putting into contrast Sherman's relative distaste for waging big, bloody battles.)

The Resaca burial ground is said to be the first Confederate Cemetery in Georgia dedicated after the war. (dd)

The Affair at Cassville

CHAPTER FOUR

MAY 19, 1864

As his engineers took up their pontoons and fired the two bridges, Johnston and his troops marched south to Calhoun, the next rail stop on the W. & A., five miles south of Resaca. On May 16, both army commanders telegraphed reports of the recent activity to their respective superiors: "I was compelled to fall back" (Johnston to Seddon in Richmond); "we will pursue smartly to the Etowah" (Sherman to Maj. Gen. Henry Halleck in Washington).

South of the Oostanaula, the topography of north Georgia no longer features tall mountain ridges of the kind at Rocky Face. Thus around Calhoun, Johnston and his engineers found no commanding terrain on which to fix a defensive line. The army consequently kept retreating to Adairsville and beyond. About this time, the story goes, as Johnston rode alongside his column a soldier called out, "General, don't fall back any farther, we are getting mighty tired."

"I am not retreating," the army commander retorted. "The enemy is on our flank and rear, and we must face the foe."

The exchange maybe apocryphal, but its telling allows for an important point. During the war, and ever since, observers have called Johnston's policy of retreating through north Georgia "Fabian." ("His infernal Fabian policy will take us all to ruin and that very rapidly," a citizen of Athens, Georgia, once complained to President Davis.) The allusion is to the Roman general Quintus Fabius Maximus, who in the second war against Carthage gave up northern Italy before the advance of Hannibal's army, falling back

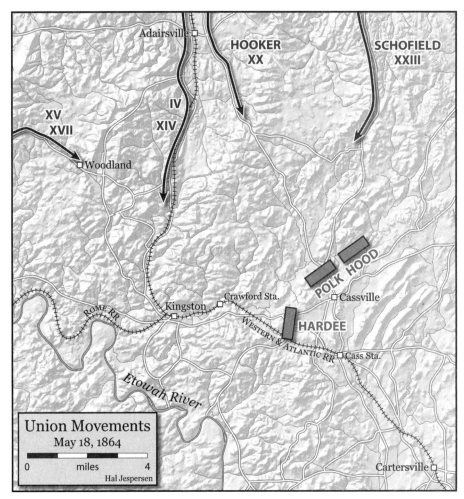

Union Movements
May 18, 1864

0   miles   4
Hal Jespersen

UNION MOVEMENTS—As Sherman's forces approached Cassville, Johnston predicted they would take two different roads, with the heavier Federal column marching on Kingston. He laid plans for Hood's corps to strike the enemy in flank north of Cassville on May 19.

on Rome and gaining strength rather than risking battle. It is said that Joe Johnston never liked being likened to Fabius because he believed the latter had had a choice in retreating; facing Sherman's army group, he believed he had no choice but to do so. Hence his purported remark to the soldier, "I am not retreating." But, of course, he was.

Sherman followed the Rebel army cautiously, through Calhoun and to Adairsville. At that place, two main roads lead on to Cassville, the next town along the Western & Atlantic, 11 miles to the southeast. One was the direct road; the longer route went through Kingston. Johnston, reaching Cassville on the morning of May 18, figured Sherman would use both roads for his marching columns. So he conceived a plan of deception and possible advantageous attacking battle.

Hardee's corps, with the army's artillery and

wagon train, would take the Kingston route, leaving a "plain, well-marked trail." Most of Sherman's forces would probably follow it. Those who did not would be approaching Cassville from the northwest. Johnston planned to place Polk's troops astride the road and Hood's corps to their right. As the Yankees approached, Polk would demonstrate against them while Hood marched out, found their left flank, and assailed it.

The plan was smart, and prospects for victory were at hand. Johnston's army was at its strongest. Major General Samuel French's division arrived on May 18, the last of Polk's Army of Mississippi, which essentially became Johnston's third infantry corps, though that designation was not made official till late July. With other reinforcements sent by the War Department from garrisons at Savannah, Mobile, and Charleston, Johnston's army was now or would soon total 73,000 officers and men—an army larger than Lee's.

Johnston's officers were aware of what other Confederate armies were doing at the time. Lieutenant General Richard Taylor had defeated Nathaniel Banks' Red River expedition in Louisiana. Lee had forced Grant to abandon the Wilderness and was handing him a bloody repulse at Spotsylvania. "News of Bank's surrender said to be confirmed," Col. Taylor Beatty, one of Hood's staff officers, wrote in his diary; "news from V-a that Lee has destroyed 45000 of Grant's army." Despite Colonel Beatty's hyperbole— the usual exaggeration of camp rumor—Lee and Taylor were in truth winning victories while Johnston was retreating. Lieutenant Thomas B. Mackall, on Johnston's staff, recorded that the situation increased hopes in the army for a victorious battle, lest it fail to match the exploits of other Confederate forces.

Thus Johnston both needed a victory and had one potentially before him if Hood could attack and whip part of Sherman's forces before the others could come up. Johnston was so optimistic—or desperate—that he issued a grandiloquent battle order, which was read to the troops on the morning of May 19. "Soldiers of the Army of Tennessee," it began, "by your courage and skill you have repulsed every assault of the enemy.... You will now turn and march to meet his advancing columns. Fully confiding in the conduct of the officers, the courage of the soldiers, I lead you to battle."

"Cheered by the success of our brothers in Virginia and beyond the Mississippi," he concluded rather pointedly, "our efforts will equal theirs."

The Cassville "pocket park," looking toward U.S. Highway 41. The big metal map set on the stone in the center, clearly showing an enemy column bearing down on Hood's flank, substantiates Hood's decision to call off Johnston's attack on May 19. (dd)

All this hot rhetoric had its desired effect. Cheers arose from every command as "'Old Joe's' ringing battle order" was read, according to one veteran.

Yet it was not to be. As Johnston had predicted, Sherman sent four of his six corps following the "plain, well-marked trail" to Kingston, engaging Wheeler's cavalry along the way. Meanwhile, Hooker's corps, with Schofield's behind it, approached Cassville on the direct road on the morning of May 19.

Union cavalry started skirmishing with Polk's troops at 8 a.m. Hood began marching to get in position for the attack. Colonel Beatty, however, noticed enemy cavalry approaching from the northeast. A perplexed Hood announced this to Brig. Gen. William W. Mackall, Johnston's chief of staff, who had just ridden up with orders for the movement. Instead of attacking the enemy in flank, Hood believed it was he who was about to be flanked, and told General Mackall he would have to call off the assault and withdraw. When an incredulous Johnston got this news, he cried, "It can't be!" But it was.

Johnston ordered Polk and Hood to fall back to a line that the engineers had sited on a ridge south of Cassville. When Hardee and his column approached, they were instructed to fall in there.

To his dying day, Joseph E. Johnston believed that Hood was lying, was fooled, or both. Lieutenant Thomas B. Mackall, nephew of the chief of staff, dutifully recorded in his journal on the 19th, "enemy in heavy force close to Hood on Canton road," as had been reported to headquarters. Yet later he added, "report of column not afterwards confirmed."

The day after the "affair at Cassville," as it has come to be called, Johnston wired Richmond, "while the officer charged with the lead was advancing he was deceived by a false report that a heavy column of the enemy had turned our right and was close upon him, and took a defensive position. When the mistake was discovered it was too late to resume the movement."

In their memoirs of the 1870s, Johnston and Hood argued over whether Hood had been duped by "phantom troops." Eventually sources appeared that vindicate Hood, including the Official Records volume carrying Union reports of the Georgia campaign (published in 1891, the year of Johnston's death, and well after Hood's). In it, Union cavalry Col. Edward McCook reported engaging elements of Stevenson's and Stewart's divisions and taking prisoners on May 19—sure signs that the Federals were not "phantom troops." In the years since, historians have weighed this and other evidence to conclude that Hood was right and Johnston wrong.

If visiting the Cassville area today, along U.S. Highway 41 you will find that the small roadside pavilion built by the federal Works Progress Administration in the 1930s supports Hood's contention. The original metal plaque has been replaced by a newer one from the Georgia Historical Commission. Its text clearly states that the approach of McCook's cavalry on Hood's flank caused cancellation of the planned Confederate attack. A painted map on the plaque shows the menacing Union column bearing down from the northeast.

The immediate impact of the "affair" fell upon Johnston's officers and men, who had been told they would be led into an auspicious battle. When they received orders instead to retreat to south of Cassville, many expressed their understandable disappointment. "For the first time the men begin to grumble and grow dispirited," a Confederate surgeon observed. Even those close to the commanding general were upset. "I could not restrain my tears when I found we could not strike," General Mackall, Johnston's loyal friend, wrote to his wife.

Brig. Gen. Edward M. McCook commanded the cavalry division that bore down on Hood's troops the morning of May 19, causing Hood to cancel Johnston's planned attacking battle. One of the 17 "Fighting McCooks" of Ohio, Edward Moody McCook was cousin of Union generals Robert L. McCook (mortally wounded August 1862), Daniel McCook, Jr., (mortally wounded at Kennesaw Mountain) and Alexander M. McCook. (loc)

NATIONAL HISTORIC SITE
ATLANTA CAMPAIGN
CASSVILLE
ON MAY 19, 1864, JOHNSTON,
ENTRENCHED ON THE RIDGE
EAST OF THIS MARKER,
PLANNED TO GIVE BATTLE
BUT SHERMAN THREATENED
HIS FLANK AND HIS CORPS
COMMANDERS OBJECTED
TO THE POSITION.
HE THEREFORE WITHDREW
TO ALLATOONA PASS.
RATHER THAN ATTACK
THIS STRONG POSITION
SHERMAN MOVED PAST IT
TOWARD NEW HOPE CHURCH.
NATIONAL
PARK SERVICE

UNITED STATES
DEPARTMENT OF THE INTERIOR

Along the Etowah River

CHAPTER FIVE

MAY 19-23, 1864

After the fizzled affair at Cassville, more bad news followed for the Rebels. On the afternoon of the 19th, Confederate infantry filed into the line laid out on high ground southeast of the town. The enemy came up and began shelling it.

In a part of Polk's sector, French's troops found they were being enfiladed—that is, hit by shells coming in from the sides of their line. Hood's sector came under cruel fire, as well. "I saw one battery of ours knocked to pieces," Brig. Gen. Arthur M. Manigault recorded, "and the gunners driven from their guns in less than fifteen minutes." General Hood and staff themselves came under enfilading artillery fire as they rode along their line. Colonel Beatty termed that ride "one of the most disagreeable" he had ever taken.

Polk and Hood met and agreed that their positions would be untenable if the enemy were to attack the next day. They took their views to General Johnston after dinner. The commanding general was reluctant to retreat, especially after having issued his bellicose general order of that very morning. But he gave in and ordered yet another nighttime withdrawal march.

Trudging along in the darkness the men became even more disgruntled. Lieutenant Mackall recorded, "troops dispirited and fagged." Mackall was especially sensitive to the mood of the Georgia troops. "All in pretty good spirits up to falling back from Cassville," he wrote, "but night retreat after issuing general order impaired confidence."

Each of the five WPA pavilions has a historical marker. This one near Cassville explains that after Hood's aborted attack on the morning of May 19, Johnston's army withdrew to a position southeast of town. The Confederates withdrew from it that night, headed for Allatoona. (dd)

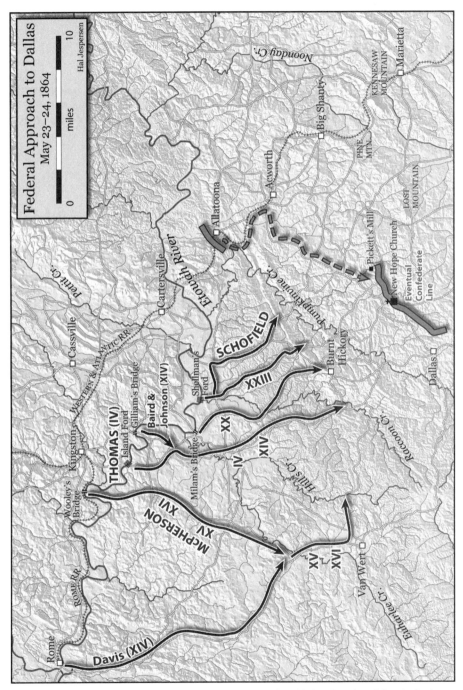

Federal Approach to Dallas—Sherman was not about to butt his head against Johnston's strong position at Allatoona. In his only departure from the Western & Atlantic Railroad, he ordered his army group off toward Dallas. The maneuver forced Johnston to take up a new line extending east from near Dallas to the farm and mill of Benjamin Pickett.

After the night march, Lt. William D. Gale, General Polk's aide (and son-in-law) recorded privately, "Gen'l J is not the man we thought him."

By most measures, morale in Johnston's army, falling after Cassville, later rose. But for many Confederates, faith and confidence in "Gen'l J." was permanently impaired. "Troops think no stand to be made north of Chattahoochee," Lieutenant Mackall confided in his journal. Colonel Beatty of Hood's staff recorded in his diary on May 20, "Reported now that we are to fall back to the Chattahoochee."

From Cassville to the Chattahoochee by crow-flight is more than 30 miles. The fact that some of Johnston's troops thought that no stand would be made between the two points was significant—and damaging for the Southerners. The mood spread all the way to Atlanta, where on May 23 Brig. Gen. Marcus Wright, in charge of the city's defenses, wired Bragg in Richmond: "indications are that Chattahoochee will be the line."

At least a few tried to be light-hearted. "Some say we are going to Florida and put in a pontoon bridge over to Cuba and go over there," recorded Capt. Samuel Foster, officer in Hiram Granbury's Texas brigade. Then he added, "while others contend that some Yankee would put a torpedo under it and blow it up."

President Davis, of course, did not join in the jollity. After he got Johnston's telegram of May 16 reporting the army's retreat from Resaca, he wired back, "Your dispatch of the 16th received; read with disappointment." He added his hope that the reinforcements recently sent to Johnston "will enable you to achieve important results."

Important results did not happen any time soon, as the Confederate army on May 20 crossed the Etowah River, the second major river barrier given up by Johnston. At least Maj. Gen. Gustavus Smith, in military retirement—having been transferred from Lee's army after Seven Pines—and serving then as president of the Etowah iron works, was able to load up and remove the plant's valuable machinery. The rearguard burned the railroad and wagon bridges after the army had gotten across, using as well two pontoon bridges as it had done five days before, crossing the Oostanaula.

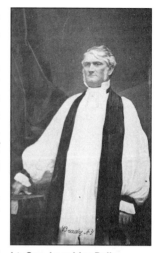

Lt. Gen. Leonidas Polk, commanding Confederate forces in Mississippi during Sherman's march on Meridian in February 1864, informed Jefferson Davis, "I see nothing left me but to fall back on Alabama." (loc)

The Etowah provided a natural defensive position for Confederates, but Johnston gave it up without a fight, puzzling many of his subordinates. (loc)

Johnston retreated to the Allatoona hills, five miles south of the river. The place was known for a 175-foot-deep man-made cut in the mountain, through which ran the W. & A. He positioned his army there, hoping that Sherman would attack him.

Old Joe would be disappointed. Sherman knew of the Allatoona hills. In the 1840s, still in the army, he had visited the area, and he was in no hurry to brush up against them now. Instead, he ordered two days' rest and refitting for his troops before the army group would head out on May 23.

Meanwhile, he called for Maj. Gen. Frank Blair's XVII Corps, part of McPherson's Army of the Tennessee, to join his forces; Blair's troops were then moving through Alabama and would join the army in two weeks. Sherman was also getting replacements and new regiments, such that he calculated he would have 80,000 men when he headed out in the next phase of his operations. For the first time in the campaign he planned to march *away* from the railroad; he therefore ordered the troops to be supplied for 20 days of operations. "The whole army must be ready to march by May 23," he ordered, "stripped for battle."

Sherman, ordinarily nervous by nature, had ample reason to be optimistic. From his headquarters in Kinston, he wrote his wife Ellen on May 22, "I have no doubt we must have a terrific battle at some point near the Chattahoochee." Yet he predicted, "I think I have the best army in the country, and if I can't take Atlanta and stir up Georgia considerably I am mistaken."

The army group commander's sunny outlook beamed down among his troops, including Israel Atkins of the 23rd Michigan, who opined that the Rebels "are as good as whipped."

They were not, of course, but their commander scarcely radiated enthusiasm. In a message to the president, Johnston acknowledged that Davis' criticism was justified. He wanted to strike the enemy, but he repeatedly deemed "an assault upon his superior forces too hazardous." Richmond officialdom, including

Secretary of War Seddon, echoed the president. "The Secretary is very dissatisfied," observed Robert G. H. Kean, Chief of the Bureau of War. "Johnston is falling back as hard as he can," Col. Josiah Gorgas of the Ordnance Department commented.

General Hood contributed to this slanderous swirl by sending his own critique of Johnston directly to Jefferson Davis. In truth, during his winter in Richmond, the president had genuinely befriended Hood. Before he left for Georgia, Davis may have asked for Hood to quietly keep him informed of Johnston's plans, having previously seen his timorous conduct on the Peninsula and before Vicksburg. Earlier in the campaign, Hood had indeed sent several letters to Richmond, criticizing Johnston for failing to be more aggressive. On May 21, Hood again wrote the president, stating only that he was sending his aide, Col. Henry Brewster, to Richmond to converse with Davis on the army's state of affairs.

Clue as to what Brewster told the president comes from Mary Chesnut, who talked with Brewster afterward. "He said Joe Johnston was kept from fighting at Dalton by no plan—no strategy." "What is the matter with him? Overcautious." "All this delay is breaking Hood's heart." "So much retreating would demoralize even General Lee's army." After this painful litany, Mrs. Chesnut concluded, "Joe Johnston disaffection is eating into the very vitals of our distracted country."

A man-made cut allowed the railroad to traverse Alatoona pass. Confederate fortifications along the hill on either side of the cut commanded the area (as best seen on the left hilltop in this photo). (loc)

DEDICATED TO THE CONFEDERATE
SOLDIERS WHO FOUGHT AND DIED
DEFENDING THESE LINES AT NEW
HOPE CHURCH MAY – JUNE 1864.
BY: GEN. WM. J. HARDEE CAMP #1397
SONS OF CONFEDRATE VETRANS

New Hope Church and the Hell Hole

CHAPTER SIX

MAY 23-25, 1864

Even before Sherman set his columns marching, Johnston received scouting reports of enemy activity 10 miles down from the W. & A. bridge over the Etowah. A look at the map and its roads pointed to the village of Dallas, more than a dozen miles southwest of Allatoona, as the enemy's likely objective. Thus as Sherman prescribed several points for his troops to cross the river, Confederate cavalry was already burning bridges there, or trying to. Johnston issued order for his army to prepare to move toward Dallas.

On the morning of May 23, when Sherman's infantry started marching, Johnston's did too. Just as General Lee at the same time was beating the Yankees to key crossroads as Grant sidled his army from Spotsylvania toward Richmond, so too (to his credit) did Johnston beat Sherman to the Dallas area. There the Confederate line was sited, six miles in length. On the 25th, Hood's corps took the right near New Hope Church; Polk the center; and Hardee the left.

Hood's sector cut right through the church cemetery. As the men dug in and built their fortifications, "the tomb-stones, the sheds, the railings around the graves were all torn away," wrote a Louisianan. General Johnston rode along Stevenson's line as the men constructed their breastworks. "He told us that the enemy were 'out there' just three or four hundred yards," remembered a lieutenant on Stewart's staff.

They were. Observers on a nearby mountain saw dust columns. Late in the morning, sharpshooters

This stone marker, set by the General Hardee Camp, memorializes the infantry of Hood's Corps, which held this sector of the Confederate line. The local S.C.V. camp sees that a Confederate battle flag flies near that of the United States. (dd)

Maj. Gen. Daniel Butterfield of New York led the 3rd Division, XX Corps until sickness sent him home for the rest of the war. He is credited for having composed the bugle call "Taps" during the Peninsula campaign. (loc)

in advance of Hood's line exchanged shots with the enemy before falling back to their main works. They brought in a prisoner who said that Joe Hooker's corps was heading their way. Thus Hood knew he was going to be attacked on May 25. The day before he had issued a general order to his troops announcing that "in the coming battle their country expects of them victory."

Hood's skirmishers had come into contact with the advance of Brig. Gen. John W. Geary's division, Hooker's corps. The firing informed Geary that Hood's corps was in his front. Geary halted while Hooker's other two divisions, Brig. Gen. Alpheus Williams' and Maj. Gen. Daniel Butterfield's, came up. The delay irritated Sherman, who remarked, "Let Williams go in anywhere as soon as he gets up. I don't see what they are waiting for in front now. There haven't been twenty rebels there today." Sherman ordered Thomas to have all three of Hooker's divisions attack without further delay.

Williams' and Butterfield's divisions formed in

The last of the five W.P.A. "pocket parks" is shown here in New Hope. A Georgia Historical Commission marker, set here in the mid-1950s, explains that Hood's Corps arrived here May 25 in time to fortify and prepare for Hooker's attack. (dd)

Hood's line ran through New Hope Church Cemetery. Soldiers entrenched; when the Yankees attacked in the afternoon of May 25, Confederates also fought from behind headstones. (dd)

columns of brigades, which meant that their front was shorter (Geary was back in reserve). The Federals' deployment negated their superior numbers, while their deeper columns meant that enemy bullets and shells would hit more men.

Hooker's troops began their advance about 5 p.m. They had to get through a mile of woods and brush before General Williams called for the double-quick. The Northerners at one point plunged into a deep ravine, which they came to call the "hell hole." Clambering to its top, they came under intense enemy fire.

The division of Peter Stewart, whose men behind their barricades and in ditches had a rather easy time repulsing the Yankee attack, manned the Confederate sector under attack. "It is fun for our troops to stand in their trenches and mow down their lines as they advance," Lt. Andrew J. Neal, serving in a Florida battery, later wrote to his sister. General

The "Hell Hole": Union soldiers had to pass through this deep ravine before climbing up the other side, straight into the musket fire of Hood's infantry. (dd)

The General William J. Hardee SCV Camp, which dedicated this monument on May 25, 2014, clearly declares the battle fought here a "CONFEDERATE VICTORY." In the Atlanta campaign, there weren't many of them. (dd)

Stewart rode behind the lines, encouraging his men. He made certain to show calmness under fire. "I am vain enough to believe that my own example inspired my men," he later wrote. When Johnston sent a message asking if he needed help, Stewart declined.

Four batteries "did great execution in the enemy's ranks," Hood reported. Brig. Gen. Williams agreed: "they poured canister and shrapnel from all directions except the rear."

Under the heavy fire, many Federals hid behind rocks and trees trying to shoot back. After two and a half hours, those able to slink back did so in the

Across the street from New Hope Cemetery are these Confederate entrenchments. The Hardee S.C.V. Camp maintains the site. (dd)

growing darkness. Hooker's failed attack at New Hope Church cost 1,665 killed, wounded and missing. Stewart lost between 300 and 400 men in what can be termed a rather small but uplifting defensive victory for the Army of Tennessee.

The Crime at Pickett's Mill

CHAPTER SEVEN

MAY 26-28, 1864

After the fight at New Hope Church, both sides spent May 26 strengthening their works, skirmishing, cannonading, and extending their lines. McPherson moved into Dallas and became the right of Sherman's line. Thomas held the center, Schofield the left. When the Federals shifted more troops eastward, Johnston sent Cleburne's division marching past Hood's flank to become the new Confederate right.

Against that very position Sherman ordered an attack on the 27th. During several hours' shelling in the morning, one of Howard's divisions, that of Brig. Gen. Thomas J. Wood, was to march behind Schofield, advance, "find the extreme right of the enemy's positon, turn it, and attack him in flank." Wood accepted the tough task, made tougher by the fact that his men had worked all night on their earthworks.

It took Wood much of the day to get into position, as he discovered that the Rebels were extending their right even as he was trying to turn it. At 3:15, Howard sent a note to Thomas that he was not sure Wood had found the enemy right. It did not matter; General Sherman was impatient for the assault to begin.

Wood dutifully deployed his three brigades, with Brig. Gen. William B. Hazen's in front and the other two behind in column. Around 4:30, Generals Howard, Wood and Hazen were discussing the assault. A staff officer had brought in a reconnaissance report: rough ground, Rebels dug in, and lots of them. At that point Wood remarked to Howard, "We will put in Hazen and see what success he has."

Hazen overheard the comment and knew its meaning immediately: his brigade would make the

The stream running along the eastern edge of the battlefield, Little Pumpkinvine Creek, is usually called Pickett's Mill Creek. (dd)

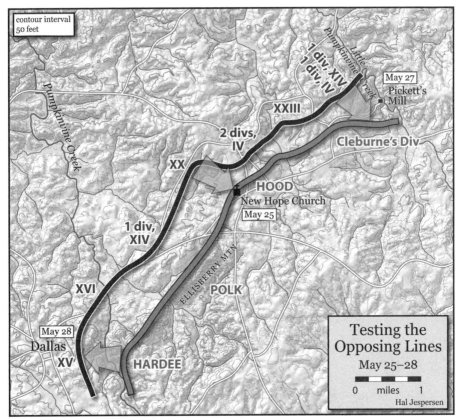

contour interval
50 feet

May 27
Pickett's
Mill

XXIII

2 divs,
IV

Cleburne's Div

XX

HOOD
New Hope Church
May 25

1 div,
XIV

XVI

POLK

May 28
Dallas
XV   HARDEE

**Testing the
Opposing Lines**

May 25–28

0   miles   1

Hal Jespersen

TESTING THE OPPOSING LINES (MAY 25-28)—Three battles were fought along Johnston's six-mile line: the Federal attacks at New Hope Church and Pickett's Mill, and Bate's assault at Dallas. All three were repulsed by the defenders.

assault alone, at least the first one, without support from the rest of the division. Hazen said not a word as he rode off to the head of his brigade. Lieutenant Ambrose Bierce was with him and after the war recalled the scene: "only by a look which I knew how to read did he betray his sense of the criminal blunder."

Hazen began his advance at 5 p.m. The Federals struggled through underbrush and up a hill taking fire from Hiram Granbury's Texans, who stood in the woods fighting without entrenchments. On Hazen's right, the Federals never got close; but on their left they broke into an open field and threatened to overwhelm the Confederates' flank until the Southerners redeployed and brought up some cavalry as reinforcements. Hazen issued the order for his men to fall back.

General Wood belatedly called another of his brigades, Col. William Gibson's, to take up the attack, but it also got shot up before making any headway. Gibson retreated, and around 7 o'clock Howard and Wood called the whole thing off, but not before another two Union brigades made half-hearted advances.

Federal casualties in the "Crime at Pickett's Mill"—Bierce's phrase—numbered 1,565 (230 killed, 1,016 wounded and 319 missing). Cleburne reported 85 dead and 363 wounded, to which could be added another 150-200 cavalrymen.

The next day the sight of so many dead men sickened Capt. Samuel Foster of Granbury's brigade: "men lying in all sorts of shapes and just as they fallen, and it seems like they have nearly all been shot in the head, and a great number of them have their skulls bursted open, and their brains running out. . . . I have seen many dead men . . . but I never saw anything before that made me sick."

Like the battle of New Hope Church two days before it, the battle of Pickett's Mill—so named for the local property of Martha Pickett, whose husband had been killed at Chickamauga—was a small-scale defensive victory whose chief importance was to raise the spirits of Johnston's soldiers.

Yet the tables were quickly turned, for the very next day Confederates suffered a sharp repulse at the other end of their line. General Johnston on the 27th had already mistaken the eastward march of Howard's columns as the start of a wholesale shift by Sherman back to the railroad. On May 28, he thought that McPherson's army at Dallas might be withdrawing in such a movement. Johnston ordered Maj. Gen. William B. Bate, whose division held the Confederate left, to feel for the enemy and ascertain his strength, "as it is believed he is not in force."

By mid-afternoon Bate announced a plan to

Maj. Gen. John A. Logan's XV Corps held the right of the Federal line near Dallas when "Grits" Bate's division attacked it on May 28. (loc)

Traces of Pickett's Mill can be seen on the west bank of the creek. (dd)

Benjamin W. Pickett (1828-1863) and his wife Martha owned farmland to the east of Dallas. A 2nd lieutenant in the 1st Georgia Cavalry, Pickett died on Sept. 19, 1863, the first day of battle at Chickamauga. He is buried in New Hope Church Cemetery, which was held by Stewart's division during the Federal attack of May 25. (dd)

his brigade leaders. On the left, Brig. Gen. Frank Armstrong's dismounted cavalry would sally forth. If they met little resistance, they would fan to the right; Bate would fire two signal cannon, and his three infantry brigades would advance and press the attack.

The plan swung into play. Around quarter to 4 Armstrong's troopers pushed forward and overran the Federal line, but were pushed back by an enemy counterattack. XV Corps commander Maj. Gen. John "Black Jack" Logan rode about and rallied his men: "Damn your officers! Forward and yell like hell!" When they did, the Southerners retreated.

By Bate's plan, that should have ended the fight. But two of his brigade commanders, worried they might have missed the cannon signal to advance, sent their soldiers forward anyway—across a field, through abatis and against an entrenched enemy.

The repulse of Bate's two brigades in the battle of Dallas was as predictable as it was costly. The engagement of May 28 resulted in 600-800 Confederate casualties to Logan's 379. General Bate, nicknamed "Old Grits" by his men, came in for some sharp criticism from them. As one Kentuckian put it, Grits was catching it "from all sides and quarters." The only positive result for the Southerners was that their reconnaissance-in-force had brought back the sought-for intelligence that McPherson still held Sherman's right strongly. But, as another Kentuckian lamented, "we paid dearly for the desired information."

Neither side made any major efforts the next day, which was spent in sharpshooting and shelling. The Federals' march back to the railroad, which Johnston had suspected, was in fact Sherman's next move. On May 30, Schofield and Thomas pulled back and started marching eastward; McPherson left Dallas the next day.

Sherman was pleased with the success of his 10-day maneuver. On June 2, after he sent cavalry to take and hold Allatoona, he wired General Halleck, "so our movement has secured to us that pass which was considered a formidable one." Sherman was more positive still in a letter home

Pickett's Mill battlefield, from the northwest corner of the cornfield looking east. (dd)

to Ellen. Johnston, he wrote, "thinks he checked us at Dallas. I went there to avoid the Allatoona pass, and as soon as I had drawn his army there,"

Sherman explained, he had maneuvered back to the railroad in "a perfect success."

Cump did not mention to his wife the two bloody repulses his troops had received at New Hope and Pickett's Mill. As we have seen (and still shall), the Union commander tended to slip unflattering details under the rug.

To their superiors, however, both army commanders summarized the fighting of May 25-28 at Dallas-New Hope Church-Pickett's Mill pretty much the same way. "Thus far we have had no real battle, but one universal skirmish extending over a vast surface," Sherman wrote Halleck. Johnston on June 1 telegraphed General Bragg that in its recent "partial engagements" his army "has had great advantage, and the sum of all the combats amounts to a battle." Bragg was not impressed, however, and a few days later told the president, "the condition of affairs in Georgia is daily becoming more serious."

After Brig. Gen. William B. Hazen got orders for his brigade to launch its assault, Lt. Ambrose Bierce remembered, "only by a look which I knew how to read did he betray his sense of the criminal blunder." (loc)

Bragg was right, but so was Johnston in claiming that the recent fighting had raised the morale of his officers and men. "Our army was never in better spirits," wrote a Mississippi artilleryman on May 29; "all seem confident of success." "The morale of the army was never better than it is now," General Mackall wrote his wife on June 3; "the men are sanguine of success and their confidence in Johnston in undiminished."

Three days later, Lt. Col. Columbus Sykes of the 43rd Mississippi, writing his wife, said the same thing: "the army is . . . ready and anxious to fight the enemy whenever 'Old Joe' gives the word."

Pine Mountain

CHAPTER EIGHT

JUNE 2-15, 1864

Confederate observers on Elsberry Mountain east of Dallas watched the Yankees moving; General Johnston rode there on June 2 to see for himself. The next day he ordered the army off toward the railroad to the next promising position, Lost Mountain, which was six miles southeast of the Dallas line.

When laid out on the 5th, the Confederates' new 10-mile-long "mountain line" extended eastward from Lost Mountain through the road junction at Gilgal Church to anchor itself on the right at Brush Mountain. The three infantry corps assumed the same order as before: Hardee-Polk-Hood.

There was another eminence, Pine Mountain, too far out in front of the line (one mile) to be included in it, but which was too commanding (300 feet high) not to be occupied. Bate's division plus artillery was put on Pine Mountain, in a salient unconnected by trenches to the main line, as if to tempt the Yankees into launching an attack upon it. Someone remarked that General Johnston was setting a trap for Sherman, and that Pine Mountain was the "Bate."

On June 3, Sherman's advance reached the railroad at Acworth, four miles south of Allatoona (and a half-dozen north of Gilgal). As he had done south of Cassville before crossing the Etowah, Sherman gave his armies some rest—this time a week. During that period, engineers rebuilt the railroad bridge across the river so that supplies could be brought south to Allatoona Station, soon to be a big supply dump for the army group. Two divisions of Frank Blair's XVII Corps arrived on June 8, replacing soldiers sick or wounded recently sent to the rear.

A Confederate veteran living after the war in Marietta, J. Gid Morris, raised money to have this tall marble shaft dedicated in 1902. Its front reads:

IN MEMORY OF
LIEUT. GEN. LEONIDAS
POLK
Who fell on this spot
JUNE 14, 1864.
Folding his arms across his
breast
He stood gazing on the
scenes below.
Turning himself around as if
To take a farewell view.
Thus standing a cannon shot
from the enemy's guns
crashed through his breast
and opened a wide door
through which his spirit took
Its flight to join his comrades
On the other shore. (dd)

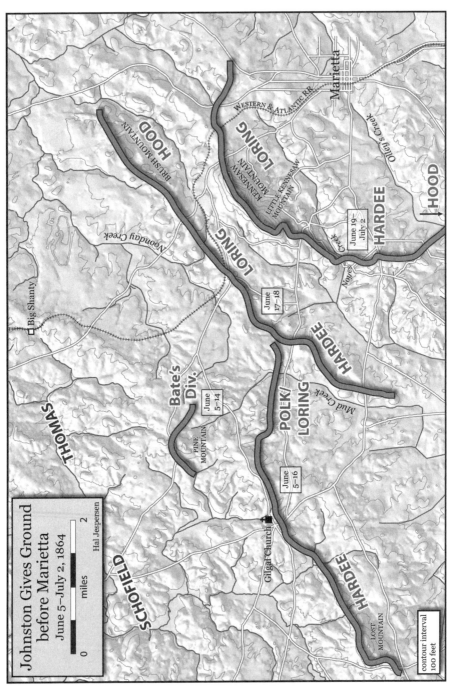

Johnston Gives Ground before Marietta—Johnston continued shifting his lines north of Marietta. Bate gave up his Pine Mountain salient the night of Bishop Polk's death there. Hardee held the left, centered at Gilgal Church for a day or so before withdrawing to the main line, which in turn was abandoned in the night of June 18-19. The army then filed into its Kennesaw line and held it nearly two weeks, while almost daily rain caused Sherman to suspend further maneuvering.

Even though Brig. Gen. John Geary, division commander in the XX Corps, claimed that it was one of his batteries whose fire killed Bishop Polk, Sherman decided that it was the 5th Indiana Battery, attached to Maj. Gen. David Stanley's division, which deserved the distinction. Brig. Gen. Walter Whitaker, one of Stanley's brigade leaders, was more specific: "a shell from the 5th Indiana Battery, commanded by Lieutenant Morrison, fired from a 3-inch Rodman gun, from the section commanded by Lieutenant Ellison, killed Lieutenant-General Polk." Ironically, Capt. Peter Simonson, commander of Stanley's divisional artillery, was killed two days later near Pine Mountain. These earthworks, behind Living Hope Church north of Kennesaw Mountain battlefield, have been identified as the 5th Indiana's position. Standing there, you can see Pine Mountain about a mile away. (dd)

With all things ready, on June 10 Sherman set forth in the next phase of his Georgia campaign. His objective was the immediate one, that of forcing Johnston's army to retreat from its mountainous position. Thus far he had in his official correspondence not mentioned Atlanta, much less informed his officers of a timetable for getting there. Yet Sherman was, as always, confident. "I think thus far I have played my game well," he wrote Ellen on June 12. A few days before, in a letter to his brother, Sen. John Sherman, the general had characterized the campaign as "a big Indian war." Thus far, he seemed to be winning it.

In their first day on the march, the Federals came upon Bate's position on Pine Mountain. They tested the Rebels' strength with musketry and artillery for the next few days while working to the east of the mountain. General Hardee began to worry that the enemy might wrap around and cut Bate off. On the evening of

Looking from Beaumont Road at the top of Pine Mountain toward the site of General Polk's death. The land is privately held, but the owner has allowed a path to be cut from the road to the monument. Visitors are asked to be respectful—no digging! (dd)

June 13, he asked General Johnston to meet him for a ride to the Pine crest the next morning to view the situation for themselves. The commanding general, conferring at his headquarters with Lt. General Polk, asked the bishop also to join the next morning's reconnaissance.

Johnston and Polk met for breakfast on June 14, then rode with their staffs to Hardee's headquarters. From there they rode to Bate's position. An officer present recalled that the generals arrived around 11 o'clock at the top of the mountain. The three generals dismounted and began their inspection of the enemy below.

At the crest was a four-gun battery commanded by Capt. Rene Beauregard, son of the famed Creole. An officer advised the generals to disperse; the enemy guns below had, the day before, found the battery's range. He was right—shells and shot began to fly and burst.

Hardee and Polk moved back. Polk tarried, taking one last look at the terrain below. Then another shell whizzed and exploded against a tree. Someone shouted that General Polk had been hit. Hardee and Johnston ran up to find their brother officer lying dead on the ground. The shell had passed clear through his body, breaking both arms and tearing open his chest.

"My dear, dear friend," Hardee grieved. A sobbing Johnston moaned, "I would rather anything but this."

Stretcher-bearers came up and placed Polk's body on a litter. Staff officers escorted it down the mountain,

Three earthen embrasures remain today at the site of Capt. Rene Beauregard's battery atop Pine Mountain. A Confederate officer, Col. W. S. Dilworth, later wrote that on the morning of June 14, when Generals Johnston, Hardee, and Polk rode up to the top of the mountain, "I asked the generals not to allow more than three or four persons with us, as a large crowd would be sure to attract the fire of the enemy." It did. (dd)

leading "Jerry," his horse. Down below, the corpse was put on an ambulance. With Johnston riding alongside, it rolled to Marietta Station, from whence the general's body was taken into Atlanta. Later that day, Johnston telegraphed Richmond: "the Army and the country this morning had the calamity to lose Lieutenant-General Polk, who fell by a cannon-shot directed at one of our batteries."

Soon Sherman knew of Polk's death from Federal signal officers—who had broken the Rebels' wig-wag code—when they waved for an ambulance to come for General Polk's body. The next day he informed Washington, "We killed Bishop Polk yesterday." After a memorial service in Atlanta, a train carried Polk's remains to Augusta, Georgia, where they were interred at an Episcopal church.

While General Johnston sought permanent replacement for the commander of the Army of Mississippi, Maj. Gen. William W. Loring took the post. Polk's death and his inspection visit to Pine Mountain led Johnston to order Bate to withdraw from his salient in the night of June 14-15. Yankees approached on the 15th and occupied the mountain.

Kennesaw Mountain

CHAPTER NINE

JUNE 15-27, 1864

Sherman mistook the Rebels' abandonment of Pine Mountain as part of a withdrawal from their entire mountain line. For June 15, he instructed each of his army commanders to press ahead and develop the enemy position.

Schofield and McPherson were to conduct turning movements on their respective flanks (Schofield, around Lost Mountain; McPherson toward Kennesaw). Thomas was to test the enemy center and, if possible, break it. These efforts met with varying success—and failure.

On the Union right Schofield's troops sortied, took a line of works, but pushed no farther. On McPherson's end, the rush by a Union brigade against Hood's sector overran a line of rifle pits, capturing several hundred prisoners before being called back.

Thomas' advance against the enemy center led to bloodier work. Geary's division moved against well-fortified Rebels on the afternoon of the 15th, incurring more than 500 casualties without any gain. To its right, Butterfield's division pushed up against Cleburne's line at Gilgal Church. The Southerners tore down the little chapel and used the wood in their fortifications. When the Yankees charged, "we repulsed them as usual," wrote one of Cleburne's officers; "we were in works." Butterfield's unsuccessful assault led to between 150 and 215 Northern soldiers killed or wounded.

On June 16, some of Schofield's troops found a position from which they could enfilade Cleburne's

Kennesaw Mountain, which looms in the background, is one of the largest "green" spaces in the Atlanta metro area. Only an hour or so from downtown Atlanta, the national park is visited each year by tens of thousands. (cm)

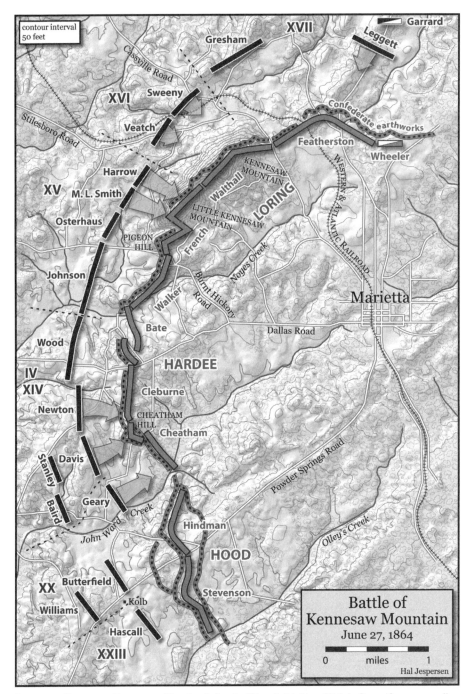

BATTLE OF KENNESAW MOUNTAIN—The Confederates' line, held June 19-July 2, ran for seven miles from east of the railroad down to the sector held by Hood's corps in front of Peter Kolb's farm. Sherman ordered a frontal assault on the center of the entrenched Rebel line on June 27.

line at Gilgal Church. They brought up artillery and started shelling. In the bombardment, one of Cleburne's brigadiers, Lucius E. Polk, lost a leg. To Cleburne's right, Maj. Gen. William H. T. Walker was literally shelled out of his headquarters. This development, added to the news that the enemy was enveloping the flank at Lost Mountain, led Johnston to decide that he would have to give up at least part of his mountain line. During the night of the 16th-17th, Hardee withdrew from Lost Mountain and Gilgal Church back to a new position west of Mud Creek, which connected with the sectors still held by Polk's (now Loring's) troops in the center and Hood's on the right.

This monument near Kennesaw Mountain battlefield reads "BATTLE OF GILGAL CHURCH/JUNE 15-17, 1864/U.S. MAJ. GEN. DANIEL BUTTERFIELD. 3RD DIV. 20TH CORPS. ARMY OF THE CUMBERLAND. C.S. MAJ. GEN. PATRICK R. CLEBURNE. CLEBURNE'S DIV. HOOD'S CORPS. ARMY OF TENNESSEE." (dd)

On June 17, the Federals skirmished and shelled "as usual," Johnston reported. Rains on the 18th prevented either side from moving, but Johnston knew that Sherman would not give up the initiative or cease his flanking tactics. "I can find no mode of preventing this," he despondently telegraphed Bragg. On the 18th, the general confessed to his wife Lydia that he had found no way to counter Sherman's "engineering system." Thus he planned for yet another abandonment of his Mud Creek-Brush Mountain position and ordered his chief engineer, Lt. Col. Stephen Presstman, to lay out a new defensive line to the south, anchoring it on Kennesaw Mountain.

During the night of June 18-19, amid heavy rains, the Confederate army slogged to Presstman's new seven-mile line. Hood's corps held the right, east of the mountain; Loring's troops manned the center ("Big" Kennesaw and Little Kennesaw) and Hardee the left. In the latter's front, to take in some high ground the line jutted out in a bulge or salient which has come to be named for the Confederate division manning it— "Cheatham's Hill."

In a little over a month, Joe Johnston had given up to the enemy more than 60 miles of north Georgia and abandoned from Dalton six separate defensive positions.

On June 15, Sherman ordered all three of his army commanders to push forward. That afternoon, Hooker's XX Corps marched down the Sandtown Road. Maj. Gen. Dan Butterfield's division encountered Confederate pickets and drove them back. But then the Federals were stopped cold by Maj. Gen. Patrick Ronayne Cleburne's entrenched infantry at Gilgal Church. "We repulsed them as usual," wrote Maj. Calhoun Benham of Cleburne's staff; "we were in works." (loc)

*   *   *

On the morning of June 19, Sherman learned of the empty Rebel works, jumped to the conclusion that Johnston was retreating to the Chattahoochee, and ordered "pursuit." Within hours, however, he realized he was wrong and, that evening, had to admit to Halleck that he had been "premature."

He ordered his force to press against the new enemy line: McPherson to the left, Thomas in the center, and Schofield the right. As he had before at Lost Mountain, Sherman called for the Army of the Ohio to maneuver around the Rebel left. Schofield probed to the south, but was halted by a rain-swollen creek. The characteristically impatient Sherman had to halt further movement till the rains stopped. Not "until we can move our army with some skill and rapidity," he told Thomas, "will there be any point in attacking the enemy."

Schofield's movement, and Sherman's past practice, led Johnston to anticipate another flanking attempt around his left. He therefore informed Hood to be prepared to march his corps from the right to the left to blunt any enemy maneuver. When Schofield began moving again, Johnston ordered Hood to start marching during the night of June 21-22. The corps passed through Marietta to a point four miles southwest of it, connecting with Hardee's left and extending the Confederate line farther to the south. Hood arranged his divisions on the 22nd with Hindman to the right, Stevenson on the left, and Stewart behind in reserve.

Hood had no cavalry, so he did not know that joining Schofield in the Federal maneuver to the southeast was part of Hooker's corps. Hooker suspected his probe would invite enemy attack; he knew it after some of his skirmishers encountered Stevenson's and brought back word that Hood's corps was in their front. Around 3 p.m., Hooker ordered his troops north of Powder Springs Road to entrench; Schofield's south of it did the same.

Without reconnaissance of the enemy position before him, Hood ordered Stevenson's and Hindman's divisions to attack. By the time the Confederates advanced, a little after 5 p.m., the Yankees ahead had dug in and brought up artillery. The resulting battle of Kolb's Farm was an easy Federal defensive victory and a bloody repulse for the Southerners. "The Shell & Shot & Miney balls flew thick as hale," recorded one Alabaman. The attack was over in an hour and a half.

Casualties for Stevenson amounted to 823; for Hindman, 215. The Union loss was well less than that, some 230.

Hood has over the years been criticized for launching a frontal infantry assault on an entrenched enemy position at Kolb's Farm. His defenders contend that because Johnston had shifted Hood's corps from his right to left precisely to stop the enemy's maneuver around his flank, Hood was simply carrying out that mission. Indeed, this is the point made by the Georgia Historical Commission roadside marker at Kolb's Farm in the Kennesaw Mountain National Battlefield Park. As a matter of record, Johnston issued no criticism of Hood for his battle of June 22, even though Hood had launched it without notifying headquarters.

These Confederate earthworks remain in the suburbs of Kennesaw, Georgia, part of Cleburne's line at Gilgal Church. The Southerners tore down the church, which was in front of their lines and in their field of fire. Granbury's Texas Brigade and Capt. Richard Goldthwaite's Alabama Battery occupied this sector. Capt. Samuel Foster, 24th Texas Cavalry (Dismounted), recorded in his diary that day: "Later in the afternoon the enemy drive in our skirmishers, and the battery men and men from our Regt. all go to work and tear that church down level with the ground in about 15 minutes. not one log left on another, even knocked the blocks, and just as the Yanks come in sight about 300 yards away they open on them with grape shot, and canister, and they soon break and run out of sight." (dd)

The fact that the commanding general continued to give Hood important assignments, as he had done from the campaign's opening days at Resaca, suggests Johnston maintained considerable confidence in him. This may have nettled the army's senior corps commander. On June 20, Hardee wrote to his wife Mary that when he had gone to Johnston's headquarters that day, "I found Hood with him. . . . Hood, I think, is helping the General to do the strategy, and from what I can see is doing most of it."

The same comity did not exist between Sherman and his senior army commander, George Thomas. The army group leader disliked the showy trappings of rank, so he belittled General Thomas' large staff and its "baggage train big enough for a division." He called the Army of the Cumberland's headquarters "Thomas' Circus" or "Tom Town." But what really got Cump was Thomas' plodding, deliberate ways, which had earned him the not-altogether flattering nickname of "Old Slow Trot." Especially when Sherman stressed keeping on the move and pressing the enemy, he became annoyed at Thomas' cautious tactics. "A fresh furrow in the plowed field will stop the whole column, and all begin to intrench," he complained.

Thomas' army, in the center of the Federal line, would nonetheless have a big role in Sherman's next planned operation. Schofield had concluded he could not press farther without overstretching his

The Atlanta Historical Society owns the small tract off Kennesaw-Due West Road where Cleburne's trench line is preserved. On a small length of it has been built this reconstruction of a well-prepared infantry entrenchment. Note the log revetment behind the earthen parapet, cross beams to support it, and raised firing platform. The second rank in the deeper ditch behind it could load muskets and hand them up to the firing line. (dd)

line. "Schofield reports he can't go ahead," Sherman spluttered, "and is far outflanked. I suppose the enemy, with his smaller force, intends to surround us."

Schofield's impasse, and the welcome cessation of the rain on June 21, caused Sherman to begin thinking of a way to break the stalemate: a frontal attack against Johnston's line. On the 24th, he issued orders for an assault to be launched at 8 a.m. on June 27, which "will endeavor to break a single point of the enemy line" somewhere on McPherson's and Thomas' fronts, while Schofield would keep maneuvering around by the right.

McPherson reconnoitered his sector for the planned attack. Big Kennesaw Mountain, rising 691 feet up, was of course impractical as an objective.

The battlefield of Kolb's Farm is part of Kennesaw Mountain NBP. Peter Valentine Kolb built this log farmhouse in 1836. A decade before the war, Peter V. Kolb II owned 600 acres of land and 10 slaves. He died in December 1863; his widow Eliza lived here in 1864. The house was damaged during the battle, but later repaired by the family. In the early 1960s, based on recollections of P. Val Kolb III, the park superintendent had the house restored to its wartime appearance. (dd)

Mac instead chose Little Kennesaw Mountain and Pigeon Hill south of it as his targets. Thomas eyed the Rebel salient ("Cheatham's Hill") as vulnerable and selected it as his assault-objective.

At 6 a.m. on June 27, McPherson's artillery opened up against Big Kennesaw. The Federals began skirmishing just to keep the Rebels there occupied. Then, at 8 o'clock, three brigades of Logan's XV Corps advanced on Little Kennesaw and Pigeon Hill. They overwhelmed a Southern skirmish line, taking 150 prisoners in Walker's division. But French's troops on Little Kennesaw, at the top of which they had two batteries, handily repulsed the enemy attack. "It soon became evident that the works could not be approached by assault," General Logan ruefully concluded.

French's division held this part of Johnston's line on Little Kennesaw. (dd)

Thomas had slightly more success on his front— but only slightly more. The Federals could see their objective, Rebel works on the high ground ahead. "I shall not come out of this charge today alive," predicted Union brigadier Charles Harker. After a brief bombardment, five brigades advanced—three from Newton's division, IV Corps, and two from Davis' division, XIV. They overran the enemy pickets and pushed on through undergrowth, some cut saplings, and the terrible fire of musketry and artillery. (General Cleburne had kept his guns masked by cut brush till the Yankees charged.) True to his prediction, General Harker, who managed to reach the parapet of

Looking from Big Kennesaw to Little Kennesaw Mountain. The top of the big mountain was not very broad; Confederates dragged three cannon up the 691-foot slope. "Little Kennesaw, being bald and destitute of timber," wrote Maj. Gen. Samuel French, "affords a commanding view of all the surrounding country." The Southerners placed nine guns on its crest. Shown on the NPS plaque is Alfred Waud's "Planting the Guns on Kennesaw," which he drew for Joseph M. Brown's The Mountain Campaigns of Georgia (1886). (dd)

the Rebel salient, was shot in the chest standing atop it. Colonel Dan McCook, of the famous "Fighting McCooks" from Ohio, fell severely wounded, but before he was carried from the field called out, "Stick it to them!"

The Northern attack faltered against the entrenched Rebels, who stood so deep in the salient that they passed loaded rifles up to the firing line. "It having been demonstrated that the enemy's works were too strong to be taken," Newton reported submissively, "the division was withdrawn." Rather than risk being shot while retreating, some Federals huddled beneath the topographic crest of Cheatham's Hill till they could safely retire.

In a sector of Cleburne's front, a brush fire erupted in front of the Confederate works, threatening the wounded Federals lying there. "Boys, this is butchery," yelled Col. Will H. Martin of the 1st Arkansas; "cease firing and help get out those men." A truce flag was raised, and soon Southerners were over the parapet helping the enemy carry its wounded to places of safety.

At 10:45, Thomas reported to Sherman that his assault had failed. McPherson did the same from his sector. Several hours later, Sherman asked Thomas if he could still find a way to get at the enemy. Slow Trot bluntly refused: "one or two more such assaults would use up this army."

Given the Union casualties on June 27, this was not quite true. Some 14,500 Northern soldiers fought in McPherson's and Thomas' attacks. By the end of the battle, 2,900 of them were killed, wounded, or missing. Confederate casualties were a fifth of that, the usual proportion of attackers-to-defenders when the latter fought from earthworks.

Sherman's casualties at Kennesaw Mountain were far less than Grant's in Virginia about that time (e.g., 7,000 at Cold Harbor, June 3), but that does not condone the commanding general's callousness toward his men's undisputed bravery on June 27. Two weeks afterward, Sherman wrote Halleck that he had ordered the attacks to disabuse the enemy—and his own soldiers—of the notion that "the assault of lines formed no part of my game." As to the cause of his failure in the battle, he blamed fate ("had Harker and McCook not been struck down so early"); but worse, he also blamed his officers and men ("had the assault been made with one-fourth more vigor").

Worst of all was his statement in a letter to Ellen: "I begin to regard the death & mangling of a couple

In the days before the Federal assault, General Cheatham ordered the artillery in his front to be masked with brush and not to reply to enemy artillery fire. Hardee's chief of artillery, Col. Melancthon Smith, later wrote, "The enemy for several days had occasionally opened with their artillery, as was their wont, previous to an attack, for the purpose of finding out the position of our batteries, and most of our division commanders would insist upon replying with the batteries on their line, there discovering to the enemy what they required; and General Cheatham was about the only division commander of our corps who agreed with me to keep them concealed until the assault was made. On this occasion, I think the wisdom of this course was proven." (dd)

In 1900, the Colonel Dan McCook Brigade Association met in reunion of veterans who had taken part in the attack on the "dead angle," Cheatham's salient. The association bought 60 acres in the Cheatham Hill area, and on June 27, 1914, the 50th anniversary of the battle, dedicated this monument to Illinois troops. This view is taken some distance away, from the Confederate earthworks. (dd)

of thousand men as a small affair, a kind of morning dash." Such crudeness may have been meant by Sherman as some perverse way of impressing his wife of his manliness. Yet one is hard pressed to find such an unflatteringly morbid statement made by any other officer on both sides during the war.

Prior to the fight at Kennesaw Mountain, Federals at Vicksburg had dug a tunnel under Confederate fortifications, exploded a ton of gunpowder and charged—only to be repulsed. After Thomas' attack failed at Kennesaw Mountain, Union soldiers—still hugging the topographic crest of Cheatham's Hill—began digging a mine in which they might eventually blow a big powder charge. The Northerners eventually withdrew before executing their plan, leaving this vestige of their digging effort, located in front of the Illinois monument. Both Federal efforts presaged the more famous mine-digging effort at Petersburg that eventually resulted in the battle of the Crater. (cm)

To the Chattahoochee

CHAPTER TEN

JUNE 28-JULY 7, 1864

Sherman accrued at least one benefit on June 27: during the fighting, Schofield had maneuvered southward so that by the end of the day he threatened the Rebel left-rear. This was the kind of development Johnston had been expecting; several days before, Lieutenant Mackall recorded in his journal, "expect to flank us on our left." Johnston thus had instructed his engineers to find another site to the rear at which to build another line when the army would have to retreat once again.

Joe Johnston took little satisfaction in reporting his victory at Kennesaw Mountain to Richmond. The larger picture involved his continued retreat through north Georgia, which he found difficult to explain. "I have been unable so far to stop the enemy's progress by gradual approaches," he admitted to Bragg after the battle, "on account of his numerous army and the character of the country, which is favorable to that method."

Johnston knew any attempt to find excuses would fail to impress the administration. Indeed, on June 24, the general's friend, Sen. Louis Wigfall, passing through on his way to Texas, visited Johnston at his Marietta headquarters and frankly warned there was scuttlebutt in Richmond that the president wanted him fired. Johnston repeated that he was unable to defeat Sherman with his own army, but suggested that if the government ordered Bedford Forrest in Mississippi to raid into Sherman's rear and cut his railroad lines, maybe that could force the enemy to retreat.

About that time, Georgia Gov. Joseph E. Brown, no friend of the Davis administration, called for

Cleburne's division held the center of Johnston's line near Smyrna Camp Ground July 3-4, and repulsed a demonstration by Thomas' infantry on the 4th. (dd)

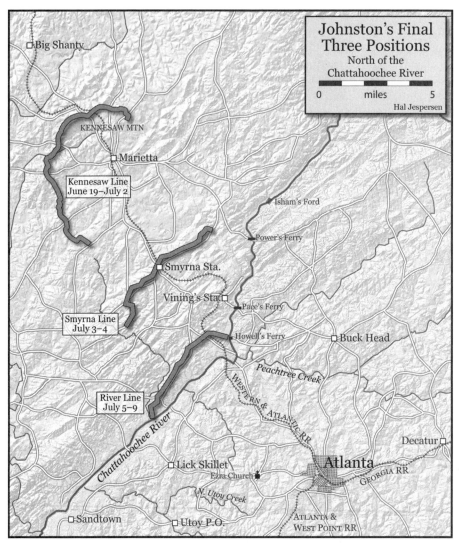

JOHNSTON'S FINAL THREE POSITIONS—Johnston knew that the Chattahoochee was his Rubicon. He strained to hold ground north of it, in the three lines that his army held from Kennesaw to the river.

the president to send Forrest's or John H. Morgan's cavalry behind Sherman's lines to save Atlanta: "this place is to the Confederacy almost as important as the heart is to the human body."

To bolster his argument, Brown enlisted the support of Georgia senator Benjamin H. Hill. Brown knew Hill would be heeded in Richmond. He asked the senator to meet with Johnston, develop with him a case for the cavalry raid, and put it in a letter to be mailed to the administration. Hill offered to go one better: he would meet the general in Marietta, learn his ideas for contesting Sherman's advance, then travel to Richmond and personally relate them to Secretary Seddon.

The senator and general met on July 1. General

FLAG OF
GENL CLEBURNE'S
DIVISION —

When William J. Hardee was promoted to major general and given command of a division, he designed a flag for it: a blue field with a silver moon in the center. In mid-1863, when the Confederate government adopted new national colors ("the Stainless Banner") and ordered that the service branches cease to use unauthorized flags, Cleburne's men protested. The administration relented, and the division kept its distinctive banner. Col. Thomas B. Roy, Hardee's chief of staff, wrote, "This was the only division in the Confederate service allowed to carry into action other than the national colors, and friend and foes soon learned to watch the course of the blue flag that marked where Cleburne was in the battle." (loc)

Hood sat in on the conference, but not Hardee. Hill asked some tough questions. If Johnston thought only a cavalry raid breaking Sherman's railroad could change the course of the campaign, why had he not sent off General Wheeler with the mounted troops under his immediate command? Johnston answered that he needed all his cavalry to scout and screen for the army. He probably did not know that on that very day Wheeler was writing Bragg, complaining that he had asked Johnston repeatedly for permission to lead a raid against the Yankees' supply lines, but had every time been refused.

Hill got to the point: given the tactical situation he faced, how long did Johnston think he could hold Sherman north of the Chattahoochee? Hill later reported that the general "did not answer this question with directness."

At the end of their conversation, Hill wanted to make certain he had the message down pat, so he carefully phrased his conclusion: "And I understand you to say, General Johnston, that Sherman cannot be defeated except by the proposed attack in his rear, and that this work must be done by Forrest or Morgan or by some such force?"

Johnston said yes.

Sherman was meanwhile pushing forward. The very flank-by-right operation that Johnston had been expecting from the enemy soon unfolded. Schofield actually marched past Hood's left, toward Ruff's Mill on Nickajack Creek. Sherman ordered McPherson to swing his army from the left, behind Thomas and to the right to reinforce Schofield's maneuver.

Southern observers on Kennesaw noticed McPherson's march on July 2 and reported it to headquarters. Johnston recognized that he would have to withdraw the army from its Kennesaw line and ordered another night-retreat to the new position, which had already been staked out seven miles to the south. This new line, six miles in length, ran from Rottenwood Creek on its right through Smyrna Camp Ground and on toward Nickajack Creek. At that point it turned to the southeast. Filing into it during the night of July 2-3, the infantry deployed as at Kennesaw: Hood-Hardee-Loring.

Johnston put the best face on his latest withdrawal in the telegram he sent Bragg on the 3rd: "The extension of the enemy's intrenched line several miles nearer the Chattahoochee than our left has compelled us to fall back six miles."

For citizens of Marietta, the sight of the army marching through town toward Smyrna was an experience "occasioning great anxiety," according to one.

Not all, however, were downcast. On July 4, a Confederate soldier penned a note to the Yankee commander that somehow made its way to him:

July 4, 1864
Mr. Sherman--
    Come on!
Yours with anxiety,
    Rebel.
P.S. We intend to give you a whipping.

* * *

While Schofield and McPherson pressed their flanking columns, Sherman intended for Thomas to close up on the new Rebel line and demonstrate against it on the 4th. The national holiday began with Northern bands playing patriotic tunes. Musicians in Johnston's army were not to be outdone; when they served up a rendition of "Dixie," Lt. George Warren of the 3rd Mississippi noticed that the angry Yankees sent over a few shells.

Fighting broke out at noon when Thomas' demonstration began. Two brigades pressed forward against that part of Hardee's line held by Cleburne's division. After overrunning the Southern skirmish line, the Federals were driven back with 270 casualties in the "battle" of Smyrna Camp Ground. Two and a half miles west, in fighting near Ruff's Mill, which again has been dignified as a "battle," a brigade of the XVI Corps charged Stevenson's division so tenaciously as to push it back to a new position, albeit incurring 140 Union killed and wounded.

Among Confederates, the day's highest-ranking casualty was Major General Hindman, who was riding through some woods when his head struck a tree branch, throwing the general to the ground. His eyesight damaged, Hindman was sent to Macon. Brigadier Gen. John C. Brown took over his division.

Thomas' and McPherson's sorties, as Sherman had intended, took the Confederates' eyes off the real development, which was Schofield's troops getting across Nickajack Creek beyond Hood's flank. There, only Confederate cavalry and Maj. Gen. Gustavus W. Smith's Georgia Militia stood before the Yankees, and they were quick to report they could not long do so. Thus General Johnston ordered another withdrawal of the army during the night of July 4-5. This one was so quickly announced that it made the city's newspapers on the 5th. "Speculation was rife yesterday to establish the reason for our retreat," announced the *Atlanta Intelligencer*, the leading daily. "To-day it is more eagerly agitated—what will we do next? Our street Generals have it that we will be flanked to the Gulf."

Sherman had, for quite a while, been thinking the Rebels would retreat to the Chattahoochee, and more than once in the last month had he believed they were doing just such a thing (as when he ordered "pursuit" early on June 19). But here he really had a point. Smyrna is just four miles from the river, and Cump very well would have asked himself what sort of experienced general, as Joe Johnston had shown himself to be, would take a defensive position so close to a river, where if his line were broken, panicky rout would send his fleeing soldiers plunging and drowning into the river.

Joe Johnston would, and did.

Two weeks before, when the army was still at Kennesaw, chief of artillery Brig. Gen. Francis A. Shoup had heard Johnston speak of having to give up the Chattahoochee as the last barrier to the enemy's advance. Mortified, Shoup offered to find a site just north of the river for one more line. To buttress it, he had in mind a different kind of fortification, in which stockade infantry forts would be the anchors of connecting rifle pits. Shoup believed his new concept of works could buy time before the army's withdrawal across the river.

Johnston snatched at his idea, and labor began on a Confederate river defense line which featured Shoup's

Maj. Gen. Gustavus W. Smith commanded the Georgia Militia during the campaign. In mid-May Gov. Joseph E. Brown ordered the militia to aid in the defense of Atlanta. Smith's force, initially 2,000-3,000, increased to about 5,000 in August 1864. Smith later described his troops: "the old men of the State up to the age of fifty-five, and the boys down to sixteen years, armed in great part with flint-lock muskets, ordinary rifles, and shot-guns." (loc)

earth-and-log redoubts, soon dubbed "Shoupades" by militia general Smith. A thousand slaves were put to work, so that eventually three dozen of the odd little forts were constructed.

As opposed to traditional earthen forts, protected by thick exterior walls of slanted dirt, General Shoup's creations featured almost vertical logs outside, built to a height of 16 feet and inner log walls also stacked up, with dirt 10 to 12 feet thick packed in between. Each fort was shaped like an arrowhead pointing at the enemy. Eighty infantrymen were envisioned as the garrison for each Shoupade. Firing platforms were provided for the soldiers to stand and repel a charging enemy.

Connecting the Shoupades were rifle pits also novel in their construction, 80-foot-high log stockades. Earthen redans for artillery were studded along the line. General Shoup laid it out so troops in each of his eponymic fortifications could deliver an enfilading fire on the next one all down the line, thus luring charging Yankee infantry into a death-trap.

Johnston's infantry marched into Shoup's new line in the early morning hours of July 5 as before: Hood-Hardee-Loring. "When the troops, accustomed to earth works, saw what they were expected to defend," Shoup remembered, "they were greatly amused and made all sorts of ridiculous remarks about them." Men in Walker's division started tearing down the Shoupades in their sector and digging the trenches they were more used to.

Generals Hardee and Cleburne defended Shoup's new works, however, and where they had been defaced, Johnston ordered their reconstruction. Headquarters even issued a circular explaining how the redoubts would form a strong line of defense. "Men better pleased," Lieutenant Mackall recorded, and settled into the line, which ran on average a mile or so from the riverbank. The railroad and wagon bridges lay behind Loring's sector. Johnston had six pontoon bridges built, two per corps, to facilitate communication and supply.

Sherman was surprised on the morning of the 5th to receive reports that Johnston's army was aligned on the north bank of the Chattahoochee. "No general such as he," Sherman had earlier predicted, "would invite battle with the Chattahoochee behind him." The army group commander quickly adapted, calling off the attack he had ordered Thomas to launch upon the enemy presumably retreating across the river. Instead, Thomas on July 5 was to draw up before the Rebel line while McPherson moved to the right. Schofield's army would head to the Union left, upstream. Cavalry were to extend the flanks probing for crossing-places: Brig. Gen. Kenner Garrard's division upstream, Brig. Gen. Edward McCook's and Maj. Gen. George Stoneman's divisions downcurrent.

Johnston's task, aside from making sure any enemy reconnaissance-in-force did not break through the line of Shoupades, was to guard the places on the Chattahoochee where enemy troops could cross. Unfortunately for the Confederates, there were more crossing-points than they could adequately guard and defend.

Once settled into Shoup's river defense line, Johnston called for entrenchments to be dug another mile downriver for infantry to cover Mayson and Turner's Ferry. To the right, Wheeler's cavalry was deployed at outposts overlooking seven ferries and fords, plus two wagon bridges (at Roswell and McAfee's six miles farther up). Downstream, Brig. Gen. William H. "Red" Jackson's cavalry fanned out 14 miles below the W. & A. bridge to guard six different ferries. All had to be on the watch. On July 3, 100 state troops had driven off Union horsemen poking around Aderhold's Ferry, 10 miles below Shoup's line.

Sherman compounded Johnston's worries by pulling out the big trick he had confidentially announced to General Grant back in April. Having outflanked the Rebels with columns sent around their left at Dalton, Resaca, Allatoona, Lost Mountain, Kennesaw, and Smyrna, as his forces approached the last river barrier before Atlanta, Sherman now planned to feint toward the enemy left but to cross on their right.

Accordingly, he ordered McPherson down the river to "display as much anxiety to cross as possible and as low down, but keep your masses ready to move to the real quarter when required." In the "real quarter"—that is, upstream—Garrard saw the Rebels had burned the Roswell wagon bridge on July 5, but he did not discern the enemy in strength across the river. "My impression is that Johnston will make no attempt on this flank," Garrard wrote Sherman late on the 7th; "his cavalry has gone to his left."

Federals downriver did their part to keep up the ruse. The Atlanta Southern Confederacy reported on July 8, "the heavy shelling at Turner's Ferry yesterday induced the opinion that the Yankees might attempt to carry that point."

Maj. Gen. George Stoneman led a cavalry division during Sherman's campaign. The year before he had commanded all the cavalry of the Army of the Potomac. After Chancellorsville, he was relieved for what Joe Hooker thought was poor performance. (loc)

The Confederate army's occupation of the Chattahoochee River line at best bought Johnston merely a few days before he would have to take the fateful step of ordering another retreat back toward Atlanta. On July 5, he telegraphed Richmond that his army now had the river at its back.

That day, in an act that conveyed the utmost pessimism, Johnston ordered all munitions machinery in the Atlanta arsenal and other factories to be dismantled, put on trains, and hauled from the city to places of greater safety. The invaluable works of the iron rolling mill, for example, went to Augusta; the percussion cap factory traveled to Macon. Army hospitals were also ordered to pack up their patients, bunks, and supplies for transport south toward Macon.

On the 6th, Johnston moved his headquarters to the south bank. He ordered the army's ordnance trains and most of its wagons there as well. President Davis responded to the general's wire of July 5 very predictably. "The announcement that your army has fallen back to the Chattahoochee renders me more apprehensive for the future," he wrote on the 7th, displaying considerable understatement. "At this distance I cant judge of your condition or the best method of averting calamity," Davis added.

Johnston, of course, had an idea on how to avert calamity, but it was the same one he had advanced before. Informing the president he had heard there were 16,000 Confederate cavalry in Alabama and Mississippi, he asked, "might not 4,000 of this cavalry prevent the danger by breaking up the railroad between the enemy and Dalton, thus compelling Sherman to withdraw?"

Poor "Old Joe." The commander in whom the

A "shoupade" today, part of Johnston's River Line. Brig. Gen. Francis A. Shoup included 36 of his earth-and-log forts in the line he had built within two miles of the Chattahoochee. Remnants of just a few of them exist in suburban south Cobb County.

(dd)

men of the Army of Tennessee had placed so much trust was indulging in unrealistic gambits at the 11th hour to force the enemy to fall back.

A month before, Capt. Sidney Champion of the 18th Mississippi had written his wife, "our beloved Genl Johnston has the confidence of almost every soldier . . . based upon skills as strategist." Now those "skills" had brought Johnston's army to within 10 miles of Atlanta, with a formidable enemy before it and a deep river behind it.

The commanding general still could not figure out what to do. On the evening of July 7, Johnston held a conference of corps commanders, including Peter Stewart, recently promoted to lieutenant general, who that day took command of Polk's/Loring's corps (Loring returned to his division). The meeting ended without consensus. Johnston would wait to see what Sherman did next.

He did not have to wait long.

Sherman Crosses the Chattahoochee

CHAPTER ELEVEN

JULY 8-13, 1864

On July 8, while Thomas demonstrated noisily downstream, Sherman ordered Schofield to find places to get his infantry across. Federals found Powers' Ferry guarded with artillery, but upstream Isham's Ferry was more lightly defended. There, a regiment paddled across on pontoons and drove off the Rebel cavalry without a single casualty. A floating bridge was soon constructed, and Brig. Gen. Jacob Cox's infantry division was marching over the water. A half-mile farther up, Northerners found a fish rock dam and simply walked across the river on it without any contest from the other side.

News of these developments, especially the enemy crossing at Isham's, was fed to Johnston's headquarters. "The Yankees are supposed to be in considerable force and of all arms," read one dispatch. That night, a Southern cavalry officer reported that the Federals at Isham's had expanded their bridgehead more than a mile to the south. "One of my men who was at that point late this evening," he wrote, "says he saw about two brigades of infantry this side of the river, with fixed bayonets, marching by fours."

This message reached HQ at 1 a.m. on the 9th. General Mackall wrote Wheeler that General Johnston was "very anxious" for more information of the enemy's crossing. Actually, he had all the intel he needed: Johnston issued orders for the army to cross the Chattahoochee. Quietly on its bridges that night, having spread sand and leaves on the spans to muffle the sound of their passage, the Southern troops

In 1864, Atlanta's city limits extended one mile's radius from today's Underground Atlanta. Since the war, the city has sprawled miles beyond. That we can today see remnants of General Shoup's earthworks in the suburbs north of the Chattahoochee is a marvel (see Mike Shaffer's appendix). (dd)

As his army retreated toward Atlanta, Joe Johnston became convinced that he could not stop Sherman's progress. He called upon the government to order Maj. Gen. Nathan Bedford Forrest (above) cavalry to raid into Tennessee and wreck the railroad supplying Sherman's forces. The Davis administration refused, arguing that Forrest in north Alabama and Mississippi was needed to protect the important agricultural resources of the Tombigbee River valley. (loc)

marched over the river. The bridges were then fired and the pontoons either taken up or destroyed. The Army of Tennessee had conducted the last nocturnal retrograde it would make under the command of Gen. Joseph E. Johnston.

South of the river, the news of Johnston's retreat slowly sank in. "I suppose they will have a great hurrahing—today," General Mackall wrote his wife on the 10th, referring to the hurrahing Yankees. "We feel much dejected and low spirited at our prospects," Capt. W. L. Trask, on Hardee's staff, entered in his journal of the 10th. Captain Wallace Howard of the 63rd Georgia had watched the army's river retreat glumly. When another officer tried to cheer him up, Howard replied, "I don't know. I don't like giving up so much territory, it looks to me like the beginning of the end and as though we were going straight down to the Gulf of Mexico."

After the Confederate army's retreat across the Chattahoochee River, both sides ceased active operations for a while. As he had done at the Etowah, Sherman ordered several days' rest for his troops before setting out again. Johnston's army encamped south of the river; engineers directed soldiers and several thousand slaves working to strengthen the city's fortifications.

In his telegram to Richmond, Johnston tried to describe his latest retreat as undramatically as he could. "On the night of the 8th the enemy crossed at Isham's, or Cavalry ford; intrenched," he wired on July 10. "In consequence we crossed at and below the railroad, and are now about two miles from the river, guarding the crossings."

The news further agitated a chief executive already in great consternation. Just a few days before, Davis had telegraphed Johnston that word of his retreat back to the Chattahoochee made him "more apprehensive." In addition, the general in Georgia was being downright stingy about sharing his plans with Richmond. With the situation crumbling daily, Davis needed an accurate report on it, so he sent his military advisor, Gen. Braxton Bragg, to Atlanta for a personal inspection.

On the very day Johnston informed the government of his Chattahoochee crossing, Sen. Ben Hill of Georgia arrived in the capital and promptly met with Davis and Seddon. Hill related details of his meeting with Johnston on July 1 in Marietta. General Johnston had been cooperative and had spoken freely, glad a prominent political figure would carry his message to Richmond. Hill emphasized how the general had asserted that only a cavalry raid by Forrest or Morgan could force Sherman to retreat. The senator also mentioned that Johnston had predicted he would be able to hold the enemy north of the Chattahoochee for at least a month.

Davis then showed Hill the telegram he had just received, relating the army's retreat across the river. Johnston had held Sherman all of 10 days from the time of Hill's meeting. The stunned lawmaker now realized Joe Johnston would have to be relieved, and offered his further help to the administration.

Hill's report was the clearest information Davis had yet received on Joseph E. Johnston's thinking, so Seddon carefully composed a memorandum recording what he and the president had heard. He then showed it to the senator, who agreed in its content but said it was not strong enough in depicting Johnston's belief that he could not defeat Sherman without help from other quarters. So Hill wrote his own memorandum of his conversation July 1. A key point was Hill's recollection of this exchange: "and I understand you to say, General Johnston, that Sherman cannot be defeated except by the proposed attack in his rear, and that this work must be done by Forrest or Morgan or some such force?" Johnston had said yes, but to make sure, Hill phrased his question two more times, to which Johnston gave the same affirmative answer. The senator had then pledged to go to Richmond to try to persuade the administration to order the cavalry raid. But news of Johnston's retreat across the Chattahoochee had changed Hill's mind. If the rest of Georgia were to be saved, Joe Johnston had to go.

Meanwhile, Johnston was giving Sherman all the time in the world to get across the river. The Confederates most certainly were not "guarding the crossings," as Johnston had claimed earlier. Rather, Johnston was allowing the enemy's seven infantry corps to build their bridges and march over at their leisure while

When Brig. Gen. Jacob D. Cox got his infantry across the Chattahoochee on July 8, Johnston was forced to withdraw his army back across the river the next day. Cox wrote the first full treatment of the Atlanta campaign for Scribner's "Campaigns of the Civil War" series. For decades Cox's *Atlanta* (1882) was the only book-length narrative of the campaign. (loc)

Capt. Orlando M. Poe commanded the engineers attached to Sherman's army group. The Federals became proficient at building trestle and pontoon bridges as the Rebels retreated across the Oostanaula, Etowah, and Chattahoochee Rivers. (loc)

Confederate engineers and their laborers worked hard on the earthworks surrounding the city.

Actually, construction of Atlanta's extensive defenses had begun long before the Yankees came, more than a year before. Captain Lemuel P. Grant, an Atlantan himself, had laid out a line of earthworks completely encircling the city, ranging a mile or two from its center. Infantry trenches with artillery forts comprised a perimeter running about 10 ½ miles in circumference. Out in front of them were cleared fields of fire, abatis, chevaux-de-frise and palisades. The works northwest of the city proved to be too close to the suburbs, so by April 1864 Grant had laid out a salient adding another mile or more of trenches with several more forts.

Much of this work was still incomplete when Sherman's forces approached, so the Southerners' energies were redoubled. On July 7, one Federal officer recorded that an African-American who had made his way into their lines said fully 4,000 slaves were toiling under the hot summer sun.

* * *

Many officers and men in the Army of Tennessee could not but help feel depressed by Johnston's retreat back to the very bulwarks of Atlanta. "We are very much disappointed in having to give up so much, such magnificent country, without fighting for it," wrote Lt.

Col. C. Irvine Walker of the 10th South Carolina to his fiancée Ada; "I should not be at all surprised if we lost Atlanta."

There are always some, of course, whose outlook is sunny. One such soldier was Joseph O'Bryan, who wrote his sister on July 13, "the army has still unbounded confidence in Genl. J. and is not at all demoralized by having to fall back so far."

A lot of Southerners were talking about Johnston's regrettable retrogrades. In the capital, Sally Buchanan Preston—daughter of a Confederate general and belle of Richmond society who was said to be engaged to marry John B. Hood—about this time told her father that Hood was far away, "backing down into the Gulf of Mexico with Joe Johnston, for aught we know."

In George Barnard's *Photographic Views of Sherman's Campaigns* (1866), this was plate 33, "South Bank of the Chattahoochie, Ga." Barnard took this view in spring 1866. The bridge across the river was rebuilt by Southerners after Federals destroyed the rail bridge on Nov. 13, 1864, before setting out on their march to the sea. (loc)

General Johnston is Relieved of Command

CHAPTER TWELVE

JULY 11-18, 1864

The political chattering class openly talked of Johnston's fate if he did not deliver a battle to drive Sherman away from Atlanta. Secretary of War Seddon told Senator Hill he favored Johnston's immediate dismissal, but that President Davis was at the time opposed to such a move.

"At the time" is important, because the situation in Georgia was becoming direr still. On July 11, Johnston telegraphed Richmond with the suggestion that the thousands of Northern prisoners confined at Camp Sumter in Andersonville, more than a hundred miles south of Atlanta, should be removed to more distant locales. Then, the next day, Johnston sent another message, repeating that he was greatly outnumbered and needed help from cavalry in Lt. Gen. Stephen D. Lee's department of Alabama and Mississippi. Joe Johnston, as we would say today, still didn't get it.

The bad news was cascading so quickly—the army's transriverine retreat, Ben Hill's report, the Andersonville suggestion, now Johnston's umpteenth call for help—that Davis had virtually concluded Joe Johnston would indeed have to be relieved. He put the idea to his most successful general, Robert E. Lee, in a telegram on July 12.

> *General Johnston has failed, and there are strong indications that he will abandon Atlanta. He urges that prisoners should be removed immediately from Andersonville. It seems necessary to relieve him at once. Who should relieve him? What think you of Hood for the position?*

Johnston 2, Hood 0. Joseph E. Johnston has two statues honoring his memory: in Dalton (1912) and on the North Carolina battlefield of Bentonville. This one was erected by the Sons of Confederate Veterans in March 2010. (dd)

This last question must have struck General Lee like a thunderbolt—but it did not come out of the blue. Especially after their meeting with Senator Hill, Seddon and Davis had evidently begun talking about relieving Johnston of his command, and logically such talk would have led to discussion of successor. Both the president and secretary remembered, just a half-year before, Lieutenant General Hardee, senior corps commander in the Army of Tennessee, had declined taking over from Braxton Bragg after Missionary Ridge. Having been offered the job once, he would not be asked again.

That left Hood, especially since he had built his fame as an attacking general. His furtive messages to Richmond since going west had also hinted or overtly stated that he favored a strategy more aggressive than Johnston's. Davis' suggestion of Hood to Lee was the upshot of all this.

That did not help General Lee, however, who in his wire from Petersburg back to the president counseled caution. First, on the proposed change of general in the middle of a campaign: "it is a bad time to release the commander of an army situated as that of Tenne. We may lose Atlanta and the army too." Second, about Hood: "Hood is a bold fighter. I am doubtful as to other qualities necessary."

That night Lee wrote a letter to the president, expanding upon his earlier points. He questioned the need at this point to change army commanders, but added, "still if necessary it ought to be done." As for Hood, he was even more skeptical than he had been earlier that day: "Hood is a good fighter very industrious on the battlefield, careless off."

"I have had no opportunity of judging his action, when the whole responsibility rested upon him," Lee wrote, carefully weighing his words on the matter of Hood's inexperience, which brought up another officer. "Genl Hardee has more experience in managing an army," Lee added.

It is quite telling that the commander of the army in which Hood had achieved fame and won repeated promotion could not now endorse his former junior officer, even though it was clear this was what Jefferson Davis was hoping for.

The next day, the president telegraphed his reply to Lee: changing army commanders was "a sad alternative," he acknowledged, "but the case seems hopeless in present hands."

If Robert E. Lee could not give the president

Born in the British West Indies, Judah Philip Benjamin grew up in Charleston, moved to New Orleans, and married a lady of Creole aristocracy. He prospered as an attorney and sugar planter. He has the distinction of being the first Jewish United States Senator (1853-1861). He served throughout the war in Jefferson Davis' cabinet as Attorney General, Secretary of War, and Secretary of State. (loc)

Jefferson Davis, the only president of the Confederate States of America, spent more than a week, July 10-17, agonizing over the decision to relieve General Johnston at Atlanta. Some historians contend that this shows Davis' indecisiveness. A case can be made, however, that the president recognized the high stakes of firing an army commander in such a strategic crisis, and that he sought the opinions of all his advisors (Lee, Bragg, the Cabinet) before making his critical decision. (loc)

what he wanted, perhaps Braxton Bragg could. Bragg arrived in Atlanta on the morning of July 13 and went straight to Johnston's headquarters. During his two-and-a-half day stay in the city, he never told Johnston why he had been sent there by Davis, explaining only that he was on an inspection tour, en route farther to Alabama (which he was). Nevertheless, General Mackall, Johnston's chief of staff, recorded, "Joe looks uneasy this morning. I am sorry to see him so fretted."

Joe had good reason to be uneasy. Bragg had barely stepped off the train when, stopping at the telegraph office near the depot, he wrote, "indications seem to favor an entire evacuation of this place."

Then he was taken by carriage to Johnston's HQ, a few miles from downtown. There he conferred with the army commander, and was confirmed in his negative first impression. Johnston had his troops south of Peachtree Creek, a tributary maybe five miles north of the city that flowed westward into the Chattahoochee, and was not contesting the enemy's crossing of the river. Wheeler reported two enemy infantry corps were on the south side. Sherman's forces were dangerously divided by a broad river,

The Andersonville National Historic Site near Americus, Georgia, features the reconstruction of a section of the stockade wall. General Johnston's suggestion on July 10 that Federal POWs there be moved to places of greater safety triggered President Davis to consider removing Johnston from army command. (dd)

yet Johnston showed no interest in attacking them. With good reason, Bragg telegraphed Richmond again that afternoon, "I find but little encouraging."

The next morning, Bragg was back at Johnston's headquarters, then visited the army's corps commanders. He spent a good deal of time with Generals Hood and Wheeler, both of whom he knew to be critics of Johnston. Bragg evidently asked Hood to put his criticisms in writing, for on the 14th Hood addressed a long letter to Bragg expressing his unhappiness with Johnston's passivity. Making such statements as "we should attack him, even if we should have to recross the river to do so," Hood was clearly saying what he (and Bragg) knew the president wanted to hear.

Yet Davis was not ready to fire Johnston, at least not without support from others in his government. That meant the Cabinet. After the war, Secretary Seddon, Secretary of State Judah Benjamin, and a couple other members recalled the meeting in which they discussed the situation in Georgia. No minutes were kept, but a good case can be made that it took place on July 14. That was a) the date Ben Hill wrote his memorandum, which Seddon told him would be shared with others; b) the day after Bragg had sent his dispirited messages from Atlanta; and c) the date Hill telegraphed Joe Johnston. Seddon had invited the Georgia senator to sit in on the meeting, and one should assume he did, for sometime on the 14th, presumably right after the Cabinet discussion, Hill still tried to be a friend of Joe Johnston. "You must do the work with your present force," Hill pleaded. "For God's sake do it."

The Cabinet members in postwar correspondence did not recall the date of their meeting, but they remembered clearly what they had said.

Seddon: "one of the gravest objections existing to

him [Johnston] was that he would not give satisfactory information or assurances" about his plans; "frank communication of his plans or assurances to the President that he would not evacuate, without making decisive battle, would have kept him commander."

Benjamin: Johnston's "nervous dread of losing a battle would prevent at all times his ability to cope with an enemy of nearly equal strength"; for this reason, Benjamin felt it was "most anxious and urgent that he should be replaced by some other commander."

What Secretary of the Navy Mallory might have said is not on record, but he later wrote in his diary that Benjamin exclaimed, "Johnston is determined not to fight, it is of no use to re-enforce him, he is not going to fight."

Ben Hill apparently spoke up at the meeting as well. Soon after the discussion, Davis had dinner with Congressman James Lyons at his Richmond home. Lyons years later wrote how the president talked about the movement to relieve Johnston: "Hill urged it on behalf of the people of Georgia and Benjamin and Seddon were so violent that they would listen to nothing."

President Davis' custom in Cabinet meetings was to reserve comment until the secretaries had had their say. At some point a vote was taken on whether to fire General Johnston: the yea vote was unanimous. Senator Hill remembered Davis' response: "Gentlemen it is very easy to remove the Genl. But when he is removed his place must be filled and where will you find the man to fill it?" Hardee was out of the question, the Cabinet agreed.

Yet despite his advisors' unanimous vote, Davis was not ready to relieve General Johnston. Doubtless, he continued to mull over Robert E. Lee's cautionary words of the 12th. Either to get the general's further thoughts, or to inform him that Cabinet members had voted to relieve Johnston, Secretary Seddon on July 15 took the 5 a.m. train from Richmond to Petersburg, there conferring with the general. Lee's views could not have consoled the president. After the war, Wade Hampton wrote he had learned Lee opposed Johnston's removal, and had said if he could not command an army "we had no one who could."

With Lee speaking on one side of the momentous issue and his Cabinet on the other, Jefferson Davis was in a fix. General Bragg had sent several telegrams from Atlanta that confirmed the situation there was worsening. Before Bragg left the city on the evening of July 15, he wired again that he had written an extensive report. It was too lengthy for telegraph, and too important to be entrusted to the mails, so he was sending it by a staff officer then boarding the train. (Also included in the packet was Hood's self-serving letter of the 14th.) But these papers would not reach Davis for several days.

The president had to act. Remembering Lee's cautionary advice, and in spite of his Cabinet's vote, Davis gave Joseph E. Johnston one more chance to save his job. "I wish to hear from you," he wired Johnston, "as to present situation, and your plan of operations so specifically as will enable me to anticipate events." Johnston's telegraphed reply was as Delphic as any he had sent to his commander-in-chief. Recounting the odds against him, he wrote,

> *My plan of perations must, therefore, depend upon that of the enemy. It is mainly to watch for an opportunity to fight to advantage. We are trying to put Atlanta in condition to be held for a day or two by the Georgia militia, that army movements may be freer and wider.*

"That was the clincher," writes one historian, and indeed it was. Judah Benjamin remembered this years after the war. "There was still hesitation," for the president to act on Johnston, "until his purpose was made to continue the retreat of his army and to abandon Atlanta to the defence of the militia; there was then an end of all doubt."

Seddon said the same: Johnston's "answer was deemed evasive and unsatisfactory, and then and not till then, under the belief that Genl. J. really meant to abandon Atlanta without decisive engagement did the President finally decide and authorize his removal."

Gustavus W. Smith, a distant cousin of Hood's, wrote his kinsman after the war about Joe Johnston's statement to Davis of July 16: "I wonder if old Joe did intend to leave my little band in charge of Atlanta whilst the three corps and the cavalry were hunting for Sherman's right or left flank. Carrumba! Wouldn't that have been a kettle of fish?"

Jefferson Davis had agonized for a week on whether to remove the commander of the Army of Tennessee. Now that Johnston had unequivocally told the government he had no plan for waging battle to save Atlanta, Davis acted quickly. Adjutant General Samuel Cooper in the War Department sent a blunt telegram: "As you have failed to arrest the advance of the enemy to the vicinity of Atlanta, far into the interior of Georgia, and express no confidence that you can defeat or repel him, you are hereby relieved the command of the Army and Department of Tennessee." Johnston was to hand over command to John B. Hood, whom the president had promoted to the rank of general.

The telegram arrived about 9 p.m. on July 17 and was rushed to Johnston's headquarters. His reaction to it is not recorded. About the same time, Hood received a wire from Richmond informing him of his promotion and appointment to army command. Years later in his memoir, Hood claimed "this totally unexpected order so astounded me," but he is not to be believed. Hood had for months been critical of Johnston and, with Bragg's help, had positioned himself to become his successor.

Hood is more credible in writing that the news from Richmond left him "deep in thought throughout the night." Indeed it should have, for Hood now faced a huge responsibility. Secretary Seddon outlined it in a separate telegram. Even though "position, numbers and morale are now with the enemy," Seddon conceded, "it may yet be practicable to cut the communication of the enemy or find or make an opportunity of equal encounter whether he moves east or west." After that, the secretary signaled that it was up to Hood to try to save Atlanta the best way he could. "You are charged with a great trust," Seddon concluded. "You will, I know, test to the utmost your abilities to discharge it. Be wary no less than bold."

The next morning, Lt. Gen. Stewart asked Hood to join him in asking General Johnston to delay transferring command until a decisive battle for Atlanta could be fought. Hardee joined them in the request. All three sent Richmond a telegram to that effect, but later on the 18th, President Davis wired back that he would not rescind his order. Hood thus took command from Johnston around 5:20 that afternoon. For his part, Johnston stayed a day or two in the city, issuing a farewell message to the army, then boarding a train with his wife for Macon.

The new army commander issued a general address to his officers and men announcing he would "bend all my energies and employ my skill" in facing the enemy.

"I look with confidence to your patriotism to stand by me," Hood declared, "and rely upon your prowess to wrest your country from the grasp of the invader."

Casualties

EPILOGUE

In the first two and a half months of the Atlanta campaign—74 days, to be exact, from May 5 to July 17—both armies had incurred significant casualties.

The Federal numbers are easier to get at. In his Memoirs, General Sherman states that during May and June his armies lost 15,829 officers and men killed, wounded, and missing. For the first part of July, probably another 3,600-3,700 Federals fell hors de combat (if one takes Sherman's July casualty figure and deducts losses from the three big battles that month). Thus approximately 19,400-19,500 Union soldiers were dead, injured or lost to the service by the time Sherman's army group got to the Chattahoochee.

Johnston's numbers are a little trickier, if only because after the campaign General Hood started arguing with him about how many soldiers Johnston lost during his time of army command. In his report, Johnston stated the army had lost 10,000 infantry and artillerymen killed and wounded. He did not mention the cavalry, but General Wheeler wrote Bragg on July 1 that he had lost almost a thousand men thus far.

Johnston also reported casualties of another "4,700 from all other causes, mainly slight sickness produced by heavy cold rains which prevailed in the latter half of June." That would put Johnston's campaign casualties around 15,700.

In addition, the Army of Tennessee's statistical return of July 10 reported 6,994 officers and men as prisoners of war—either captured or deserted. Adding this roughly 7,000 men to the former number,

Of the more than 450 soldiers' graves at Resaca, 424 are marked "Unknown." (dd)

Confederates killed in the battle of Resaca, May 14-15, 1864, are buried in the Resaca Confederate Cemetery. Dedicated in October 1866, this was the first graveyard established in Georgia exclusively for Southern soldiers. The plaque on the right stone column pays tribute to Mary J. Green, who led the initiative to establish the cemetery, based on two-and-a-half acres of land given by her father. (dd)

one counts Johnston's toll of casualties incurred by mid-July to be about 22,700.

...which is the figure Hood came up with in his campaign report. "The Army of Tennessee lost 22,750 men, nearly one-third of its strength," he wrote, during the 74 days of Johnston's command.

Hood backed into this number another way. He took the army's peak strength (70,000), deducted the effective number of officers and men he inherited (47,250), and presto: Johnston lost 22,750 soldiers!

It got worse. A decade later, writing a response

Andrew Reynolds of the 89th Illinois is buried at New Hope Church. (dd)

to Johnston's memoir in a New Orleans newspaper, the Times, Hood rounded out the number to a full 25,000. He repeated the claim in Advance and Retreat, in which he inserted his Times article.

Historians' discussion about Johnston's casualties is far from over. A recent apologist for Old Joe, Steven H. Newton, posts his number of K W M as 14,213. Richard M. McMurry, Hood's biographer, has repeated his subject's contention of 25,000 soldiers lost before July 18.

Stay tuned....

It's hard to visit an old cemetery in north Georgia and not come upon headstones of Confederate soldiers. This one stands in New Hope Church Cemetery. (dd)

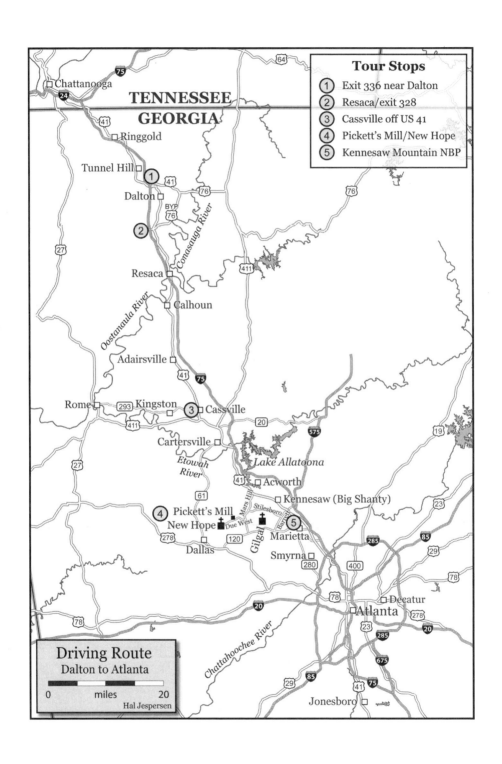

Tour Stops

1. Exit 336 near Dalton
2. Resaca/exit 328
3. Cassville off US 41
4. Pickett's Mill/New Hope
5. Kennesaw Mountain NBP

TENNESSEE
GEORGIA

Chattanooga

Ringgold

Tunnel Hill

Dalton

Resaca

Calhoun

Adairsville

Rome   Kingston   Cassville

Cartersville

Oostanaula River

Conasauga River

Etowah River

Lake Allatoona

Acworth

Kennesaw (Big Shanty)

Pickett's Mill
New Hope   *Due West*   *Stilesboro*

Dallas   Marietta

Smyrna

Chattahoochee River

Decatur

Atlanta

Jonesboro

Driving Route
Dalton to Atlanta

0   miles   20

Hal Jespersen

Driving Tour

A TOUR OF THE ATLANTA CAMPAIGN, FROM DALTON TO KENNESAW MOUNTAIN TO THE CHATTAHOOCHEE RIVER

Because of the winding routes of the armies, which twisted through the mountain passes as they paralleled the railroad, a chronologically smooth driving tour becomes difficult. Beginning in Dalton, where Joseph Johnston assumed command, we have tried to put together a tour that offers readers an opportunity to see as many relevant sites mentioned in the text as possible. Each tour stop contains a cluster of related sites to visit.

At Dalton

The Civil War community in Dalton makes the claim that Whitfield County, Georgia, has more undisturbed Civil War earthworks than any other county in the United States. The local preservation organization, Save the Dalton Battlefields, LLC, is doing a great job in identifying and working to protect many of these works.

An example is **Mill Creek Gap Battlefield Park.** From Atlanta, drive north on I-75 to Exit 336. Cross the interstate heading west on U.S. 41. Drive 0.8 miles. The park is on the left, in front of the Georgia State Patrol office.

In the late 1930s the U.S. Department of Interior and the New Deal Works Progress Administration (WPA) teamed up to create five roadside pavilions ("pocket parks") along U.S. Highway 41. The first

This is one of two statues to Confederate General Joseph E. Johnston in the country. Dedicated in 1912 by the United Daughters of the Confederacy in downtown Dalton, its inscription hails Johnston for having "directed the 79 days campaign to Atlanta, one of the most memorable in the annals of war." (The other statue was dedicated on the Bentonville, NC, battlefield in March 2010.) (dp)

is about a mile south of Ringgold (with a fine bronze statue of Pat Cleburne).

The second is at Dalton, here in front of the State Patrol building. A stone-based pavilion features an informative metal plaque with map showing the opposing armies' positions in the opening days of the campaign. Several historic markers placed here in the 1950s by the Georgia Historical Commission also explain the area's war history. One explains that George Disney of the 4th Kentucky (Lewis' "Orphan" brigade) was killed atop Rocky Face Ridge and buried where he died. His grave was discovered in 1912 by Boy Scouts, who set a marker there. (A path leads up the ridge—but only the hale and hardy should hike to the top. Disney's grave is actually beyond the crest.)

Facing the State Patrol building, look to the left of the parking lot for sign "Mill Creek Gap Battlefield Park." A short walk up the hill leads to the earthworks of the Confederate Fort Fisk, occupied by the Eufaula Battery and Gibson's Louisiana brigade.

Via Rt. 41 S, cross back over I-75 at Exit 336. Drive east 0.7 miles to Willowdale Rd. Turn left on Willowdale, 0.6 miles to Crow Valley Rd. Turn right on Crow Valley Rd. Watch for sign, "Historic Marker," where you will turn left onto gravel road. Drive down road to end to the water treatment plant. Dalton 150th has placed a colorful plaque on **"The Battle of Mill Creek Gap, May 7-12."** Text and map are by Robert D. Jenkins, President of Save the Dalton Battlefields.

Turn left back onto Crow Valley Rd. to its dead end/T intersection. Turn right onto Poplar Springs Rd., then .5 mile to **Poplar Springs Baptist Church.** A Georgia Civil War Heritage Trails plaque in the front of the church parking lot explains the fighting here in Crow Valley, May 9-12, when Schofield's XXIII Corps probed the right of the Confederate line, held by Hood's Corps.

Captain Van Den Corput's Confederate Cherokee Battery site is on the hill behind the church. Walk past the three white crosses into the woods and follow the trail to these impressive earthworks.

Back via Rt. US 41 S (east) into Dalton. Right onto Thornton. Left on Hawthorne.

Cook-Huff-Boring House. 314 N. Selvidge St. at corner of Selvidge and Hawthorne. General Johnston's headquarters in December 1863-March 1864 were located here. In the dining room to the rear of the house, Maj. Gen. Cleburne read his proposal advocating the arming of slaves for Confederate military service. A Georgia Historical Society marker in the front yard explains the event.

Fort Hill. South on Selvidge; turn left on Waugh. Right on Glenwood Ave. Turn left on Fort Hill Street. Georgia Civil War Heritage Trails plaque is at the top of hill in front of Fort Hill School. Georgia Historical Society marker explains that the 14th USCT on August 15 helped drive off Wheeler's cavalry. On October 14, the same regiment held this fort until compelled to surrender. Many of the black Federals were returned to slavery. When ordered by the Confederates to join in the work of tearing up railroad track, one African-American soldier refused and was shot.

Joseph E. Johnston statue. North on Glenwood to Waugh; turn left. Cross the railroad; left on Hamilton. Statue is downtown, at Hamilton and Crawford Streets. Dedicated in 1912 by the local

The Clisby Austin House, near Tunnel Hill. Sherman had his headquarters here May 7-12. During this time he learned of McPherson's failure to seize the railroad at Resaca. (dd)

The Western & Atlantic Museum is located at 215 Clisby Austin Road in Tunnel Hill, Georgia. The museum conducts tours of the tunnel, which is otherwise locked to pedestrians. (dd)

Joe Johnston's headquarters were here at the Huff house in Dalton. On the evening of Jan. 2, 1864, at a conference called by Johnston, Maj. Gen. Pat Cleburne read his proposal that the government arm slaves as soldiers for the Confederate army, with the promise of emancipation upon Confederate victory. (dd)

chapter of the United Daughters of the Confederacy, the monument inscription praises Johnston for having "directed the 79 days campaign to Atlanta, one of the most memorable in the annals of war."

South to Cuyler Street; turn right. Drive five blocks west of Thornton to **West Hill Cemetery**/Confederate section and memorial wall. Note at entrance marker to Johnston's grand review of the Army of Tennessee near here, April 19, 1864. Confederate soldiers' section is toward the rear of the cemetery. Georgia Historical commission marker, mid-1950s, mentions 421 unknown Southern soldiers buried here. Since then, researchers have been able to name 452 interred Confederates. In April 1999, the Civil War Round Table of Dalton erected a marble monument to the soldiers buried here.

The Confederate monument in back of the soldiers' section was dedicated in the 1890s—a marble soldier in kepi and overcoat standing with musket at rest.

Dug Gap State Battlefield Park. South on Thornton to Walnut Avenue; drive west back over I-75 at Exit 333. West on Dug Gap Battle Road 1.7 miles up the mountain. State park is on the right. Federal forces made two assaults against the gap, February 25 and May 8. Both were intended as demonstrations: February 25 to deter Johnston from sending troops to Mississippi while Sherman was conducting his Meridian campaign; and May 8, while McPherson was marching toward Snake Creek Gap, aiming to outflank the Rebel army's position.

At Resaca

From Dug Gap, back to I-75 south. We recommend Exit 328; drive east to US 41 S. Six miles south, turn left on Chitwood Rd.

Van Den Corput battery site. At 323 Chitwood, stop at "Battle of Resaca" GHC marker, to

Johnston kept his headquarters here at the Huff house (314 N. Selvidge Street) until March '64 when he moved them to the Tibbs house on Hamilton Street. (dd)

The Huff house was undergoing interior restoration at the time of our visit in October 2015. When reopened, visitors will be led to the parlor in which General Cleburne read his famous proposal. (dd)

left of road. The earthwork embrasures of Capt. Max Van Den Corput's Cherokee Battery are on private property, but the owner will allow a small group to view them. Do not park in the driveway. Walk up past residence on right; note the driveway cuts through a Confederate infantry trench. Walk past home at end of driveway. Five embrasures are ahead of you.

Back to US 41 S. About a half-mile south, at green sign, "Confederate Cemetery," just beyond Confederate Cemetery Road on left is the **WPA pavilion/"pocket park" #3,** explaining the action at Resaca.

Turn onto Confederate Cemetery Road. At end is the **Resaca Confederate Cemetery**. Note on the right side of the stone entrance arch is a WPA tablet to Resaca resident Mary Green. After the war, she led efforts to disinter Confederate soldiers from the battlefield and rebury them here. Twenty unknown Southern soldiers are arranged in concentric circles.

Entrance to the Resaca Battlefield Historic Site, off Interstate 75 at exit 320. At the time of this writing, the 500-acre park, located in Camp Creek valley, is scheduled to open in May 2016. (dd)

Fort Wayne. After the Andrews railroad raid showed the Western & Atlantic Railroad's vulnerability, Georgia troops constructed fortifications on the north side of the Oostanaula to protect the railroad bridge. Today the 65-acre tract is owned by the county. Definitely worth a visit! (dd)

South on US 41 into Resaca; turn left on GA 136. Turn right onto Taylor's Ridge Road at sign for Faith Deliverance Church to **Fort Wayne historic site**, county-owned 65 acres. Walking trail leads to earthworks of Fort Wayne, named after Confederate Brig. Gen Henry C. Wayne.

Back on 41 S; right onto 136. West across I-75 to **Resaca Battlefield Historic Site** in Camp Creek valley. Pavilions and markers line the drive, which parallels I-75. Walking trails have also been marked out.

South of the river on US 41; turn into Gordon County Sheriff's complex for Georgia Civil War Heritage Trails marker, **"Oostanaula River Bridges."** Text describes the retreat of Johnston's army across the Oostanaula during the night of May 15-16.

US 41 south through Calhoun and Adairsville, some 20 miles' drive (I-75 is quicker, but much less scenic). Approaching Cassville Road, look to left for **WPA roadside pavilion/ "pocket park" #3.** Turn left onto Cassville Road. Park is on left. The original plaque on the granite platform has been replaced by a newer Georgia Civil War Commission tablet, with a map showing McCook's cavalry division bearing down on Hood's right flank. The unexpected enemy approach forced Hood to call off the attack Johnston had hoped to deliver on May 19. In plaque text, note after acceding to cancellation of Hood's attack, Johnston ordered the army to retreat to a ridge east of Cassville, where he and engineers had laid out a defensive line.

At Cassville

Turn left out of pavilion park onto Cassville Road. Before stop-sign intersection with Cassville-White Road, park on right side for **WPA marker (1936), "Site of Cassville."** Note that the town was named for Lewis Cass, who would sit on the Georgia Supreme Court in the 1840s. Cassville was the seat of Cass County. After the death of Savannah Col. Francis S. Bartow at Manassas, the state legislature renamed it Bartow County; Cassville became Manassas. In 1864, Sherman's troops burned the town. The Georgia Historical Commission marker gives the date as Nov. 5, 1864. But Capt. Charles Wills of the 103rd Illinois recorded in his diary that on Oct. 12, 1864, after Federal soldiers found the bodies of nine comrades presumably killed by guerrillas in the area, troops burned the town. Its destruction was so complete it was never rebuilt.

Turn right onto Cassville-White Road to Cassville Cemetery. Drive up the hill to the rear of the cemetery. Although there is no marker, this is **the ridge along which Johnston had pitched his line on the afternoon of May 19.** That night, after Gens. Hood and Polk complained that their sectors were being enfiladed by enemy artillery, Johnston reluctantly ordered another retreat—this time across the Etowah River, to the heights around Allatoona Pass.

Down the slope are the graves of some 300 Confederate soldiers. In the center of the section is a tall stone obelisk, dedicated in 1878. The inscription includes, "It is better to have fought and lost, than not to have fought at all." Nearby is the grave of Confederate Brig. Gen. William T. Wofford (1824-1884).

Not too far from the Cassville "pocket park" is this marker with a plaque from the W.P.A. in the 30s, stating that in the fall of 1864 Northern soldiers burned the town of Cassville— then named Manassas, after the first Confederate victory— to the ground. (dd)

At New Hope Church

From cemetery exit, turn right back onto Cassville-White Road, which intersects with Interstate 75 (Exit 296). Drive 27 miles down I-75 S to Exit 269, Barrett Parkway. Turn right onto Barrett, heading west. Approx. 3 miles from interstate, turn right onto Stilesboro Road. About 1 ¼ miles, turn left onto Kennesaw-Due West Road. After about 3 miles this becomes Due West Rd. Take Due West into New Hope.

WPA pavilion/ "pocket park" #5. Dallas-Acworth Rd. and Bobo Rd. The metal plaque explains the "New Hope Church Phase of Atlanta Campaign." After testing Johnston's lines here on May 25, Sherman eventually moved his forces east back toward the Western & Atlantic.

GHC marker, "The March of Hardee's Corps, May 23-25, 1864," states that Hood's corps reached New Hope Church on May 25 in time to fortify and repel Hooker's attack that afternoon. "Polk's March to Lost Mountain" pertains to the

Confederate fortifications at New Hope Church thwarted Joseph Hooker's Federal attacks. (loc)

Confederates' eastward march ca. June 4.

Across the street, the Gen. William J. Hardee Camp of the Sons of Confederate Veterans maintains a section of Confederate rifle pits and raised the monument.

Drive across to the New Hope Church Cemetery. Confederate soldiers are interred there from the battle of May 25. In the southeast corner of the cemetery is also buried Lt. Benjamin Pickett, killed at Chickamauga, owner of the farmland called Pickett's Mill.

Pickett's Mill Historic Site, maintained by the state of Georgia, offers an undisturbed battlefield within an hour's drive of Atlanta. (dd)

From the cemetery turn left and left again onto Old Cartersville Road. Turn right on Bickers Road and park. The **"Hell Hole" ravine** is across Old Cartersville Road from Bickers Rd./ Johnston's Way subdivision. The Atlanta History Center owns the land where Federal troops faltered in their advance against Hood's line to the south, but has not placed a marker.

At Pickett's Mill Battlefield

From New Hope, drive east on Dallas-Acworth Rd. about 1.5 miles. Turn right onto Pickett's Mill Road at the GCWHT sign arrow. At dead end turn right onto Mt. Tabor Road.

Pickett's Mill State Battlefield Park is at 4432 Mt. Tabor Rd., Dallas. The Visitor Center features an engaging museum and 12-minute film on the battle. Three walking trails allow several hours' enjoyment of pristine earthworks and terrain very much like that of 1864.

At Gilgal Church

From Pickett's Mill, south on Mt. Tabor. Turn left onto Due West Road; becomes Kennesaw-Due West Rd. where Due West turns right. Two blocks east, Gilgal Church is on the left.

Confederate earthworks occupied by Cleburne's division parallel the road. A section of them have been renovated to show replica of an infantry parapet.

GHC marker, "Due West Community," states that the church was destroyed here in fighting, mid-June '64. Confederates dismantled the building for wood to use in their fortifications here.

At Pine Mountain

East on Kennesaw-Due West Road to Stilesboro Road; turn left. Two miles north is Living Hope Church at Mack Dobbs and Stilesboro Roads. Park in church lot. Path enters woods from back of parking lot. Follow meandering path to **5th Indiana Battery earthen embrasures.** Look southwest toward Pine Mountain; Capt. Peter Simonson's artillery fired from here the shot which killed Lt. Gen. Polk.

Back onto Stilesboro Road; head south. After a short distance turn left on Beaumont Road. Drive up Pine Mountain to the GHC marker on the right. The property is private. Asking that there be no littering or relic-digging, the owner allows groups to use the Georgia Power footpath from the roadside marker to the **Rene Beauregard battery embrasures and monument** to General Polk. Here, on June 14, 1864, Polk was examining the enemy positions below in company of General Johnston and Hardee. Captain Beauregard warned the officers to disperse, as the Yankees had earlier found the range of his position. Polk lingered, and was struck by a shell and instantly killed. Three embrasures remain; the fourth was leveled in the grading of the lot downhill for the homeowner's yard.

In 1902 Marietta resident and Confederate veteran Gideon Morris raised this stone tribute to Polk. Note on its north face, "Veni vidi vici 5 to 1." Back then, convention held that during the war 600,000 Confederates battle 3,000,000 Federals—hence the "5 to 1."

If you visit Big Kennesaw on a clear day —which we didn't when taking this shot —you can see as far away as Stone Mountain, nearly 30 miles to the southeast. (dd)

At Kennesaw Mountain

The National Park Service sponsors a variety of educational programs for visitors, including living history demonstrations. (cm)

South on Stilesboro Road to **Kennesaw Mountain National Battlefield Park.** Elaborate Visitor Center holds museum, bookstore and theater for feature film on the campaign and battle of June 27. A driving tour map of the park, based on the NPS's tour route, follows on pages 118-119.

After the war, the Col. Dan McCook Brigade Association bought 60 acres of land at Cheatham Hill; McCook was mortally wounded in the battle of June 27. The Illinois monument there was dedicated in July 1908. Congress established the Kennesaw Mountain National Battlefield Site in 1917. A local association was formed and bought 450 acres, including Big and Little Kennesaw Mountains. Today's park includes 2,882 acres.

During the spring and summer, buses carry visitors to the top of Kennesaw Mountain, with its several embrasures for Confederate cannon. On a clear day you can see the skyline of Atlanta off to the southeast.

From the mountain top, a hiking trail leads a mile to Little Kennesaw Mountain, site of earthworks for two Confederate batteries. A round-trip walk back to the top of Big Kennesaw takes about an hour.

From the Visitor Center, following the helpful map in the park brochure: Stilesboro Road/Old Mountain Road to Pigeon Hill. Markers explain this part of the Union attack; out in field is a monument to the 3rd U.S. Infantry Regiment.

During the Civil War Sesquicentennial in 2014, 2.1 million people visited Kennesaw Mountain National Battlefield Park. (cm)

Burnt Hickory road; turn right onto Whitlock/ Dallas Highway; turn left to Cheatham's Hill. A walk along the Confederate trench line takes one to the "Dead Angle," the salient in which Sam Watkins' Tennessee and other regiments in Frank Cheatham's division repulsed the enemy attacks.

Out of driveway; turn left back onto Dallas Highway/left onto John Ward Road; left at Cheatham Hill Road. On right, Sherman/Thomas headquarters. During the afternoon of June 27, when Sherman considered further action, Thomas bluntly stated to Sherman "one or two more such assaults would use up this army."

Right on Cheatham Hill Road. Cross Powder Springs Road and right to Kolb's Farm. Site of attack by two of Hood's divisions, June 22. Hood has been criticized for ordering the charge, but the GHC marker gives him the benefit of the doubt: "The extension of the right wing of Federal forces S. of the Dallas Rd., threatening to outflank him, Johnston sent Hood's Corps from the right, (E. of Kennesaw) to this, the extreme left, with directions to stop further Federal advances."

Back to Whitlock Avenue; drive east toward Marietta. Take Marietta Parkway/120 Loop to I-75. South on I-75 for four miles; watch for signs to I-285. Turn onto 285 west. Exit Bankhead Highway. Turn right on Oakdale Road for **Johnston's River Line**. For details, see Michael Shaffer's excellent Appendix in this volume.

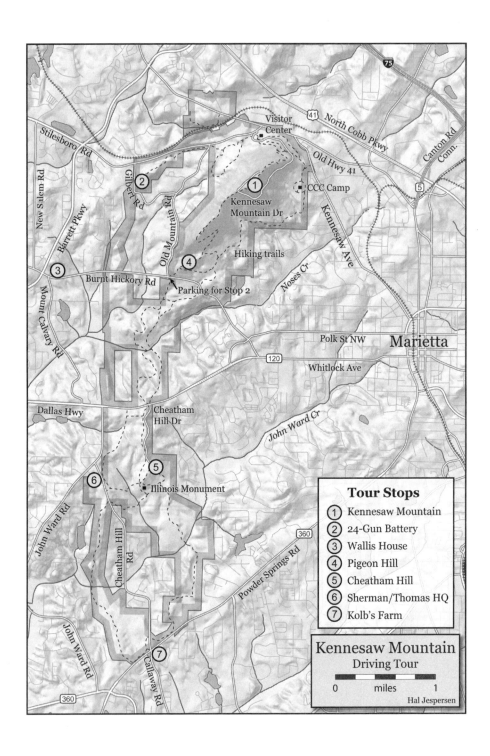

Tour Stops

① Kennesaw Mountain
② 24-Gun Battery
③ Wallis House
④ Pigeon Hill
⑤ Cheatham Hill
⑥ Sherman/Thomas HQ
⑦ Kolb's Farm

Kennesaw Mountain
Driving Tour

0   miles   1

Hal Jespersen

The National Park Service's driving tour offers seven stops within the national park. The park also has 19.7 miles of hiking trails. A museum in the park's visitor center offers an excellent overview of the campaign. Quoted material below comes from the park's driving tour map.

1) Kennesaw Mountain—Accessible by a short but moderately steep trail or by bus, the top of the mountain offers views southeast toward Atlanta and northwest toward the "Georgia terrain where Sherman's and Johnston's armies struggled in the late spring and early summer of 1864."

2) 24-Gun Battery—"Located on a small, wooded rise facing Little Kennesaw and Pigeon Hill, this Federal gun emplacement accommodated four batteries, each containing six artillery pieces. These guns bombarded Confederate forces on Kennesaw Mountain off and on for days." The Park Service notes this stop is "undeveloped."

3) Wallis House—Union General Oliver Otis Howard used this home as his headquarters after owner Josiah Wallis vacated it when the armies arrived. Wallis built the house in 1853. Sherman visited the building during the battle at Kolb's farm.

4) Pigeon Hill—"A foot trail leads to Confederate entrenchments on this mountain spur, where one of Sherman's two major attacks was repulsed."

5) Cheatham Hill—Some of the park's most impressive earthworks stand atop this salient in the Confederate line. "The fiercest fighting of the battle raged here at what came to be called the 'Dead Angle,'" the Park Service says. The Illinois monument, the largest on the battlefield, is accessible by a short walking trail.

6) Sherman/Thomas Headquarters—Here, Sherman and Thomas developed their orders for an assault against the Confederate position occupied by Gen. William Hardee atop Cheatham Hill.

7) Kolb Farm—"On the afternoon of June 22, 1864, Union soldiers repulsed Confederate General Hood's ill-fated attack just north of Power Springs Road. Union General Joseph Hooker used the Kolb House for his headquarters after the fight. The Kolb family cemetery is adjacent to the house."

Also of interest to hikers is the original Civilian Conservation Corps camp located on the east side of the mountain. In Marietta itself, visitors may wish to stop at the Confederate cemetery (final resting place for 3,000 Confederates) and the Marietta National Cemetery (final resting place for 10,000 Federals). "Henry Green Cole donated the land as a join Confederate & Union cemetery, hoping to heal ill feelings between the North and South," says the Park Service. "His vision was never realized, and the Union and Confederate cemeteries remains Separate." The Marietta Museum of History is also located downtown and the Southern Museum of Civil War and Locomotive History is in the nearby town of Kennesaw.

Marking the top of Kennesaw (cm)

The Battle of Pickett's Mill: Evolving Presence

APPENDIX A
BY STEPHEN BRIGGS

After retreating across the Etowah River in May 1864, Confederate Gen. Joseph E. Johnston and the Army of Tennessee settled into the Allatoona Mountains, a natural defensive position. Union General William T. Sherman opposed directly assaulting Johnston there. Sherman decided instead on a flanking movement, crossing the Etowah River 16 miles west of the Allatoona mountain range and moving away from his supply line, the Western and Atlantic Railroad, concentrating his forces in Dallas, Georgia. Sherman's initial goal was to move around Johnston's left flank and possibly cut off or isolate Johnston before moving back towards the Western and Atlantic Railroad, and Marietta. The Western and Atlantic was a supply line for Johnston's army, as well, linking his army with Atlanta. Johnston, aware of the Federal movement thanks to his cavalry, moved his army west to counter the Federals, resulting in the three battles in Paulding County, New Hope Church on May 25, Pickett's Mill on May 27, and Dallas on May 28, 1864.

On May 27, 1864, 14,000 Federal troops from the Army of the Cumberland under the direction of Maj. Gen. Oliver Otis Howard's IV Corps, with elements of the XIV and XXIII Corps, fought against troops mostly from Maj. Gen. Patrick Cleburne's division from the Army of Tennessee. Cleburne had a combined strength of around 9,000 men including around 1,000 from Brig. Gen. John Kelly's dismounted cavalry division. Unfortunately for Howard, he was unable to use his numerical superiority to his advantage. Howard was also unaware of the strong Confederate position, believing he was attacking the extreme right of the Confederate line where it was supposedly vulnerable. In reality, Howard was charging the Confederate center, held mostly by veterans, including Hiram Granbury's brigade of Texans and Daniel Govan's Arkansas brigade, both from Cleburne's division. Cleburne was fully aware of the Federal presence in the area.

Much of Pickett's Mill Battlefield is covered by forest—a main reason its earthworks are so well preserved today. (dd)

The Federals faltered for various reasons: the attack was conducted piecemeal; it came in column formation (impractical in the unforgiving terrain of Paulding County); and it started around 4:30 p.m. (late for Civil War battles). The first sortie came from Brig. Gen. William B. Hazen's brigade, which immediately became separated in a deep ravine—one half going into the ravine, the other half joining a desperate struggle in a cornfield. Following in succession were Brig. Gen. William B. Gibson's brigade then Col. Frederick Knefler's brigade. Knefler was only to support an orderly retreat from the first two failed attacks.

Colonel Benjamin F. Scribner deployed to support the Federal left and was ordered to advance in cohesion with Hazen in the ravine, from the top of a small wheat field. Scribner found difficulty advancing due to Kelly's Confederate cavalry, harassing the Federals and impeding their progress. In addition, elements of Confederate Brig. Gen. William Y. C. Humes's division from the First Tennessee, under Col. James T. Wheeler, were able to cross Pickett's Mill Creek, also slowing down Scribner's advance. After finally clearing the Confederate cavalry from across the creek, Scribner was too late to support the attack in the ravine. On the Federal right, near a large wheat field, Brig. Gen. Nathaniel C. McLean's brigade was supposed to support that end of the Federal line; McLean was reprimanded for his performance during the battle and later transferred.

In order for the Federals to turn the Confederate right flank, they had to clear troops from in and around the southern end of the cornfield and, if plausible, roll up the Confederate right. However, the Federals found themselves in a pincer movement in the cornfield, surrounded and unable to overcome the Confederate forces, only going as far as the field's northern end, considered the high tide of their advance. "General Granbury saw the threat to his flank and immediately sent to Govan for help," writes historian Brad Butkovich.

Govan assisted by sending Col. George F. Baucum's 8th and 19th Arkansas and, eventually, Brig. Gen. Mark P. Lowrey's brigade to secure the right. He then sent Brig. Gen. William Quarles's brigade from Lt. Gen. Leonidas Polk's Corps to help.

Pickett's Mill has the uniqueness of being the scene of a night attack, too, which came at around 10:00 p.m. Many of the Federal troops trapped in the ravine feared being shot in the back if they retreated;

they feared being shot or captured if they advanced. Granbury's brigade suddenly charged them, and more than 200 ended up as prisoners, including some 70 wounded.

Cleburne gave praise to Granbury's brigade: "It needed but the brilliance of this night attack to add luster to the achievements of Granbury and his brigade in the afternoon. I am deeply indebted to them both."

"The intense battle was a clear-cut Confederate victory, with Union losses estimated at 1,600 and Cleburne's at 450," summarizes one historian. "However, the battle only checked the Federal advance and prevented the turning of the Confederate right flank. It did not alter the outcome of the Atlanta Campaign."

This state historical marker at the battlefield states that the result of the Confederate defensive victory here was "a few days' delay" in Sherman's approach to Atlanta. (dd)

The battle of Pickett's Mill is notorious for being unspecified in Gen. William T. Sherman's memoirs. Those directly involved in the battle from both sides express a contradictory view to Sherman, describing the difficulty of the terrain, confusion, and ferocity. Marcus Woodcock of the 9th Kentucky Volunteers, of Knefler's brigade defines the difficulty of the terrain that the Federals had to endure, also mentioning his anxiety prior to combat and his wound: "Across deep hollows and through almost impenetrable thickets of undergrowth . . . our line was ordered to lie down, and there we remained for a few moments suffering from the most terrible anxieties known to the soldier, knowing that you will in a moment have to participate in it. . . . [A]bout sundown I was struck on the right thigh by a ball which penetrated the flesh."

Adding to the destruction was Confederate Capt. Thomas J. Key's two 12-pounder howitzers, detached from Hotchkiss's Battalion, pouring solid shot and canister into the densely packed Federals. Cleburne cited Key for his gallantry and effectiveness: "[I]n the fiercest part of the struggle he ran his battery by hand to within sixty yards of the enemy's lines."

Hazen's topographical engineer, Lt. Ambrose Bierce, best described the unsureness of sending in

Hazen's unaccompanied brigade: "Only by a look which I knew how to read did he betray his sense of the criminal blunder."

In the 1930s through the 1950s, battlefield aficionados Beverly DuBose, Wilbur Kurtz, and later Philip Secrist certainly knew of the location and importance of Pickett's Mill. In 1973, the state of Georgia finally purchased the land, yet even by the 1980s, Pickett's Mill did not have its own distinction in commemorations and was simply compiled into the histories of the battles of Dallas and New Hope Church. Ironically, today Pickett's Mill has fared better than both New Hope and Dallas as far as battlefield preservation is concerned. In 1992, the state opened a park here. Historian Brad Butkovich offers an assessment most visitors agree with: "The Battlefield today is one of the most if not the most well-preserved battlefields of the Civil War."

Although Pickett's Mill is receiving more exposure today, many still remain unaware of its location or significance. However, for the Sesquicentennial in 2014, the reenactment of the battle of Pickett's Mill attracted a large audience. James Wooten, chief historian of Pickett's Mill State Historic Site, states that the Sesquicentennial at Pickett's Mill "drew over a thousand spectators compared to the 500 that had been predicted to attend."

Pickett's Mill is certainly gaining more recognition today, hosting annual events such as reenactments of the battle and candlelight tours in November that sell out. Throughout the rest of the year, there are living history demonstrations and lectures. The nearby church, it seems, is not the only location with "new hope."

Stephen Briggs *of Cobb County, Georgia, is a graduate of Kennesaw State University. He earned an M.A. in public history and museum studies, directed by Dr. Keith Bohannon of the University of West Georgia. Steve is presently interim director of Pickett's Mill State Historic Site.*

Cleburne's troops did not have a chance to dig in before the Yankees charged. These Confederate earthworks were constructed after the battle. (dd)

My Time with "Company Aytch:" Personal Memory and the Kennesaw Line

APPENDIX B
BY ROBERT W. NOVAK

There are many times I remember driving to Kennesaw Mountain as a child. It was a favorite spot for my parents and me, even as an infant and toddler, my mother and father taking walks along the major trails that make their way through the park. The first real house I ever lived in was built very near the property line of the park, and home videos and photos exist of my father and I walking ahead of my mother, my small hand clutching his pinky finger, while my father explained the battle to me. Of course, I do not remember a word of what my father said, but his stories must have hooked me somehow. Kennesaw Mountain has always held a special place in my heart, and I frequently walk the trails and battle lines of the Federal and Confederate armies that called the area home for weeks.

The mountain must also hold power for others—some who are there for history and many more for jogging and dog walking. Most have only the faintest idea of what happened on the ground around them more than 150 years ago, and some go so far as to climb up and over the well-preserved earthworks. Unfortunate as the situation is, I can find comfort in the fact that the people of Marietta and Kennesaw are still visiting the park and, while they may not know the order of battle nor the troop movements or the casualty figures, they are still experiencing the land for what it is: beautiful and home.

The war in 1864 does not resonate with much of the Civil War community. It is hard to find glory in nine and a half months of grinding, siege-like warfare around Richmond and Petersburg, or nearly 24 hours of constant fighting in the rain and mud of Spotsylvania. The monumentation of those battlefields (or lack thereof) alone sends a powerful message about how and if the soldiers themselves wanted to remember those places. Unlike the field of Pickett's Charge, for example, there were not tens of thousands of

The Kennesaw Mountain National Battlefield, as one of the largest "green" spaces in the Atlanta metro area, draws tens of thousands of visitors a year. (cm)

Is young Bobby Novak's father preparing to load him into a cannon during an early visit to Kennesaw? (m)

people marching and waiting at Kennesaw Mountain's 150th anniversary celebration. For local Georgians and for some visitors, however, Kennesaw Mountain, Pigeon Hill, Kolb's Farm, and Cheatham Hill all resonate as powerfully as the rolling fields at Gettysburg.

In 1882, Sam Watkins, formerly of Company H, the "Maury Gray's," First Tennessee Infantry, published his now famous memoir, Company Aytch. Having fought in nearly every battle of the Army of Tennessee, Sam Watkins found himself outside Marietta, Georgia, in June 1864. His regiment had been consolidated with the 27th Tennessee earlier in the war and was positioned in a salient of the Confederate line near the Kolb farm. Unbeknownst to Watkins at the time, his position would come to be known as the "Dead Angle" for the horrific fighting that would take place on June 27, 1864.

Watkins recalled in vivid language his experience fighting on that day. He claimed that, after his regiment had abandoned the line a few days later, he came to a stream where he was going to bathe himself, only to find his right arm "battered and bruised and bloodshot from my wrist to my shoulder, and as sore as a blister." He claimed that he had fired 120 rounds on June 27, frequently having to exchange his gun for one of his comrade's. Watkins remembered how desperate the fighting was, frequently alluding to the closeness of the Federals, one of whom crested the earthen bank of the Confederate line, waving the Federal flag, only to be gunned down to the calls of "Look at that Yankee flag; shoot that fellow; snatch that flag out of his hands!"

He mentions singed hair and clothes from the Federal guns right in their faces, blood of wounded and dead comrades spurting into their faces while blood "gushed" out of their ears and noses from the concussion of the guns—"my pen is unable to describe the scene of carnage and death," Watkins wrote.

The most dramatic event of all is Watkins' description of the death of his "more than friend" William A. Hughes. Watkins had killed two Federals at extremely close range when another "rushed up" on him saying, "You have killed my two brothers, and now

Sam Watkins's famous memoir Co. Aytch served as the basis for Don Oja-Dunaway's song "Kennesaw Line." (w)

I've got you." As the Federal soldier put pressure on the trigger, Hughes grabbed the muzzle of the musket, taking the round through the hand and arm.

The reader can feel the conflicting emotions of Watkins' memories. He struggles to create a coherent narrative, frequently jumping back and forth from fight to fight, suggesting the difficulty in remembering his experiences. As the book was written nearly 20 years after the fight at Kennesaw, Watkins makes sure to include references that bring the reader out of the moment, such as calling the national colors that stood over him "the beautiful flag of the Stars and Stripes," and frequently referring to the gallantry, bravery, heroism, and ultimate salvation of the men who were killed and wounded in the fighting. While the basic premise of Watkins's account follows all the guidelines of a glorious fight—an outnumbered and disadvantaged foe holding back swarms of enemy soldiers, desperately trying to hold onto their position—the details described above show a much darker, grislier story.

Civil War musician Bobby Horton has kept "The Kennesaw Line" alive for buffs. (cm)

However, it is the former notions of glory, bravery, and sacrifice that singer/songwriter Don Oja-Dunaway referenced when writing his most famous song, "Kennesaw Line," which he wrote in the 1960s and which he recorded on his 1989 album *Kennesaw*. Oja-Dunaway was a St. Augustine staple, often playing at "The Milltop" and was one of the "revered 'real Florida' folk talents." There was a time, however, when he was a surveyor in Atlanta, Georgia, where he was frequently uncovering artifacts. He became an avid reader of Civil War history, and the lyrics to "Kennesaw Line" would suggest that Sam Watkins' Company Aytch was among the most influential:

Well the sun rose high above us that morning
On a clear and cloudless day
A peckerwood, he tapped on a tree
That would soon be shot away
The heat blistered down through the leaves on the trees
The air seemed hot enough to catch fire
Heaven seemed to be made of brass
The sun rose higher and higher

This is taken almost directly from the beginning of Watkins' section entitled "Dead Angle." The song continues with the final two-thirds being a fictional

Late in the war, Confederates began conscripting younger and younger men—but not so young as little Bobby Novak. (m)

conversation between "Sammy" and his "old mess mate, Walter Hood":

And then everything got real still and quiet.
My old mess mate, Walter Hood
Said, "Them boys down there they're up to something
I know it ain't no damn good"
Well it was then the storm broke, swept down on us
Rumbling through the hills
Walter sighed and he dropped his rifle
I heard him say something 'bout whippoorwills

He said, "Sammy, can't you hear 'em singing
Singing for you and me
Yes, and all the Maury Grays, Lord
Carry me back to Tennessee
God bless the First and the Twenty-seventh
The Grand Rock City Guard
Sammy, nobody ever told me
That dying would be so hard."

Sammy, I think I'm hurt real bad.
Ain't this a hell of a day.
You'd best go and leave me now.
I think I need time to pray.
You know how bad I been wantin' to go home,
But I couldn't see rightly how.
Colonel Feild ain't gonna have a choice this time.
Guess I'm gonna get my furlough now.

He said, "Sammy, can't you hear 'em singing
Singing for you and me
Yes, and all the Maury Grays, Lord
Carry me back to Tennessee
God bless the cowards and the brave alike
Who died where the seeds of death are sewn
And I pity those poor Yankee bastards
Who died so far from home.

Watkins does mention Walter Hood along with Jim Brandon in the same section that he recalls what happened to "William A. Hughes, my old mess mate and friend." A listener can easily discern that Oja-Dunaway wanted to encapsulate the glory and honor exhibited by the men of the 1st, 27th Tennessee on June 27, 1864, following the lead of Watkins in his post-war memory. However, Watkins' account includes many descriptions that would encapsulate the in-gloriousness of war.

Nevertheless, "Kennesaw Line" has been sung by many prominent folk artists, the most famous of which was Bobby Horton, who recorded it for *Songs of the CSA, Vol. 2*, released on July 18, 1986. Horton is an avid Civil War enthusiast, growing up in the midst of the Civil War's Centennial in Birmingham, Alabama. In 1984, he was asked to produce a song for a film set in 1863 Indiana, the research for which uncovered hundreds of Civil War-era songs that turned into 14 volumes of what his website calls "authentic Civil War tunes."

Four men have connected to Kennesaw in four completely different ways. I was a local who grew up walking the same ground that men like Sam Watkins claimed could not be adequately described with a pen. Two others were singer-songwriters whose passion for the Civil War led them to record and create music set in the period. Each also has their own memory of Kennesaw Mountain, as do the thousands of visitors that the park receives every day. The position Sam Watkins and the men of his regiment held is still visible today, as are the Federal lines not 20 yards from the Confederate parapet. A monument dedicated to the men of Illinois who fought and died at the "Dead Angle" looms large atop Cheatham Hill, one of the handful dotting the battlefield.

For many visitors to that spot, however, they walk past it, utilizing the trails that zig-zag through the park on jogs or dog-walking exercises. Part of me is angry that they do not know what happened where they walk— but they are creating their own memory for Kennesaw Mountain, one that animates the continually evolving memorial to the men who fought and died there.

Robert Novak (fourth from right) continues his appreciation for Kennesaw and the experience of the men who fought there. (m)

ROBERT "BOBBY" NOVAK *is a Civil War historian who has called the Kennesaw area home for 20 years. He is currently working towards a master's degree in history from West Virginia University and hopes to continue on to receive his Ph.D.*

The Chattahoochee River Line Today

APPENDIX C
BY MICHAEL K. SHAFFER

Returning to Georgia 10 years after the armies marched across the state during the Atlanta campaign, civil engineers J.T. Dodge and H.H. Ruger mapped the defensive positions built during the Civil War. On the Cobb County side of the Chattahoochee River, they captured the various features of the Chattahoochee River Line.

Brigadier Gen. Francis Asbury Shoup, General Joseph E. Johnston's artillery chief in the Army of Tennessee, developed the idea for a series of fortifications that stretched for around six miles. The northern anchor rested above the Western and Atlantic Railroad bridge crossing of the river, and the southern terminus extended below the Mayson-Turner Ferry Crossing. Shoup formed the idea for the position and received Johnston's approval to begin construction almost 10 days before the June 27, 1864, Battle of Kennesaw Mountain.

Designing a unique set of aboveground fortifications, which resembled three-sided log cabins minus a roof, Shoup oversaw the work crews, which included 1,000 impressed enslaved persons. When Maj. Gen. G. W. Smith first saw the positions, he labeled them "Shoupades," probably a play on the creator's last name and the traditional stockade term commonly used during the war. The Dodge-Ruger map marked 36 Shoupades intact in 1874, and although estimates vary on the number built, one certainty exists: nine Shoupades remain today.

During metropolitan Atlanta's expansion in the 20th century, much of the River Line fell to progress, as new highways, residential areas, and industrial parks permeated the area. Thanks to the efforts of an early pioneer in the history of the region, Wilbur Kurtz, and the later work of local historian William

Confederate earthworks are seldom seen in metro Atlanta beyond Fort Walker, shown here in Grant Park southwest of the city. The ongoing preservation of what's left of General Shoup's line north of the Chattahoochee is therefore that much more important. (dd)

The Confederate trench Line at Discovery (ms)

Scaife, portions of the River Line received recognition and escaped further encroachment.

Realizing the need to preserve, protect, and interpret the remaining segments of the defenses, the idea of the River Line Historic Area (RLHA) came to life in 2000. Working with the Mableton Improvement Coalition, and involving a body of interested parties, the RLHA continues this work today. Beginning in 2013, and continuing into 2014—through a grant from the National Park Service—work on a battlefield preservation plan began in earnest. A series of public forums took place to gather input and collect ideas on increasing the awareness of the Chattahoochee River Line. The goal: make the area engaging for all and create a destination for heritage tourism.

Completing the report in 2014, the results focused on two primary locations along the River Line, both on Cobb County-owned property. Five of the nine remaining Shoupades rest on public property, the balance on privately owned land. One location, Shoupade Park near Smyrna, contains two of the Shoupades, has interpretative signage and remains open to the public. River Line Park, site of one Shoupade, also has signage and access via a walking trail. At least one Shoupade rested on the Atlanta side of the river; this position remains today, although inaccessible, on property the City of Atlanta owns. The fifth Shoupade, found at Discovery Boulevard, sits on a 103.4-acre tract, which Cobb County owns. This site marks one of the focal points for future access and interpretation. The Discovery site, placed on the National Register of Historic Places (NRHP) in 1973, contains one Shoupade, almost 1,500 feet of Confederate trenches, a two-gun Federal artillery redan, and rifle pits.

In Georgia, a Special Purpose Local Option Sales Tax (SPLOST) program exists, allowing each county

Michael K. Shaffer, *a Civil War historian, author, lecturer, newspaper columnist, and instructor, is a member of the Society of Civil War Historians, Historians of the Civil War Western Theater, and Georgia Association of Historians. Shaffer frequently lectures to various groups, and currently teaches Civil War courses at Kennesaw State University's College of Continuing and Professional Education.*

to levy a special sales tax to gain funds for public projects. Voters go to the polls, as they did in 2014, and vote on these SPLOST projects. If approved—and in 2014, Cobb County voters favored the ballot—the money raised will go toward specific programs. The 2016 SPLOST contains $1 million for work at Discovery. The project calls for building a full-sized Shoupade, installing interpretative signage, creating access trails, and added parking. A unique part of the Discovery design rests in a planned monument to honor all African-Americans, who aided both armies in building earthworks and fortifications. Based on research conducted during preparation of the preservation plan, no monument of this type exists elsewhere today.

Another Cobb County-owned section of land, 23.7 acres on Henderson Road, occupies a second focus in the plans for the River Line. The battlefield preservation plan marked this tract for listing with the NRHP, an action completed in June 2015. The Henderson property contains Federal earthworks and two artillery redans (10th and 15th Ohio Batteries). Similar to Discovery, the plan calls for improving access to the property, installation of interpretative signage, and creating a public picnic area.

Pondering "why the position should not have been held indefinitely," Shoup carried the abandonment of his 1864 creation to the grave. The RLHA continues with efforts to resurrect the story. To follow the progress of the plans detailed in this appendix, visit www.riverline.org.

The western artillery redan at Henderson Road (ms)

Federal Logistics During the Atlanta Campaign

APPENDIX D
BY BRITT MCCARLEY

One of the least understood aspects of the Atlanta campaign is the logistical system that supplied William T. Sherman's three Union armies (i.e., an "army group") on the march to the Gate City of the South. From early May to early September 1864, the Federal Armies of the Cumberland, the Tennessee, and the Ohio—altogether about 113,000 men and 254 artillery pieces—fought Gen. Joseph E. Johnston's roughly 55,000-strong Confederate Army of Tennessee, commanded in the latter half of the campaign by Gen. John B. Hood. Chiefly, the struggle was for control of north Georgia and Atlanta, the Deep South's principal transportation, manufacturing, and administrative center. This appendix focuses on Union supply during the campaign as one of the keys to Sherman's capture of Atlanta.

Preparing his army group logistically for the march took Sherman, his staff, and the supply officers and railroad officials in his Military Division of the Mississippi about six weeks to complete. After meeting with newly promoted Lt. Gen. Ulysses S. Grant, now the Union army's general-in-chief, and together devising the North's grand strategy for defeating the Confederacy once and for all, Sherman himself took control of the logistics preparation process.

Three railroads formed the system's backbone: the privately owned Louisville & Nashville Railroad (RR), the army-operated Nashville & Chattanooga RR, and finally the State of Georgia-constructed Western & Atlantic RR—in all upwards of 1,000 miles of railroad run principally by the army's U.S. Military Railroad (USMRR) agency. In addition, Louisville, Kentucky, functioned as the campaign's base of

Chattanooga had always been an important rail juncture, but it became an essential hub for Sherman's push into Georgia. Lookout Mountain looms in the background. (loc)

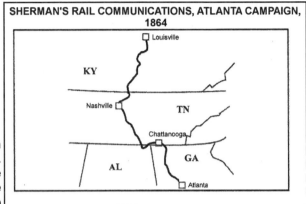

SHERMAN'S RAIL COMMUNICATIONS, ATLANTA CAMPAIGN, 1864

Sherman's supply line began as far north as Louisville. The farther into Confederate territory it ran, the more security became a concern. (bm)

operations; Nashville, Tennessee, served as its forward base; and Chattanooga, Tennessee, operated as its advanced depot. From Chattanooga southward, the USMRR transported supplies to the farthest railhead, which was often very near the fighting front and occasionally even drew Confederate artillery fire.

Sherman and his logisticians calculated that for supplies to accumulate in quantities sufficient to begin the campaign, especially in Chattanooga's plentiful and spacious warehouses, no less than 130 railroad cars—each carrying 10 tons of such commodities as ammunition, food for both soldiers and animals (about 60,000 horses and mules), medical supplies, uniforms, and general equipage— would have to arrive daily at the advanced depot. It was a Herculean task, and Sherman quickly proved that he was unafraid of inconveniencing and even annoying anyone to finish the job on time, including estranging Unionist east Tennesseans whom the army had been feeding rather than see them go hungry.

Sherman also severely limited both small-unit transportation and individual baggage. A mere 5,000 army supply wagons and 900 ambulances operated between the railheads and the trenches. Not simply content to issue instructions for others to pare down encumbrances, Sherman lived by his own words. Writing to the Union army's quartermaster general on the campaign's eve, he asserted that "my entire headquarters transportation is one wagon for myself, aides, officers, clerks, and orderlies. . . . Soldiering as we have been doing for the past two years, with such trains and impediments, has been a farce, and nothing but absolute poverty [on the march] will cure it."

By early May, warehouses from Louisville to Chattanooga all but burst with supplies. During the first week of that month, both parts of the Union's main effort against the Confederacy began their marches south. Accompanying the Army of the Potomac in Virginia, Grant started from his northern Virginia winter camps on the overland trek toward the Southern capital at Richmond. From Chattanooga and surrounding areas, Sherman did the same for the march to Atlanta.

Throughout the Georgia campaign, which followed the approximately 140 rail miles of the Western & Atlantic RR from Chattanooga to Atlanta, Sherman's armies drove their Confederate opponents, often strongly fortified on high ground, steadily southward, using flanking movements more so than battles. The Federals' greatest logistical challenge during the roughly 12 weeks of marching and fighting was keeping the railroad all the way back to Louisville functioning and free of Rebel guerrilla raiders and cavalry forces.

During the campaign's opening moves, Sherman's army group maneuvered through Snake Creek Gap and forced Johnston's army south from Dalton to Resaca, Georgia. There the two sides fought the first battle of the campaign for two days in mid-May along the Oostanaula River. After the Federals crossed the river downstream and thereby threatened the Western & Atlantic, Johnston so hastily withdrew that he failed to completely destroy the railroad bridge over the Oostanaula. Before

Confederate failure to destroy Tunnel Hill gave Sherman's supplies a "free pass" into northwest Georgia. (loc)

the march southward could resume, the bridge had to be repaired. The **USMRR** Construction Corps' Colonel William W. Wright estimated four days to complete the work, which would use the bridge's thankfully undamaged stone piers as the foundation to build upon. Impatient by nature and especially now so near the campaign's start, Sherman responded, "Sir, I give you 48 hours or a position in the front ranks." Using mostly locally-cut timber to speed the reconstruction process—which became standard practice for the rest of the march to Atlanta—Wright split the difference at three days, and Sherman forgave the tardiness.

Despite numerous attempts to sever the Union supply line, the railroad continued to operate successfully. (bm)

Sherman's armies crossed the next major river, the Etowah, in late May, left the life-giving railroad behind by heading southwest, suffered the campaign's first Union supply shortages as a result, and by early June through maneuver and battle had regained the all-important Western & Atlantic south of the river in the nearby Allatoona Mountains. Using the same techniques as at the Oostanaula, Wright's Construction Corps rebuilt the destroyed Western & Atlantic bridge over the Etowah—resulting in a massive span 600 feet long and 67 feet high—in only 5.5 days, and trains bearing much-needed supplies reached the fighting front soon thereafter.

Rain for most of June slowed the Union pace to a crawl, imposed worse shortages than before as supply wagons bogged down in roads turned to quagmires, and led to Sherman's disastrous decision to directly attack Johnston at Kennesaw Mountain on June 27. Fortunately, dry weather returned about then, and soon Sherman's army group surged forward and flanked Johnston out of his magnificent Chattahoochee River Line by early July. As the Confederates withdrew south of the Chattahoochee, they thoroughly destroyed the Western & Atlantic railroad bridge but again left the vital stone piers in place. Drawing once more on their experience at both the Oostanaula and the Etowah, Wright's bridge builders took 4.5

The United States Military Railroad ran across the Chattahoochee, allowing Sherman's army group to supply itself after it had jumped the last geographic barrier to the city. (bm)

days to erect one of the North's greatest military engineering feats of the war: a span 780 feet long and 92 feet high! Supplies would thus remain uninterrupted all the way to the Union trenches for the final push toward Atlanta.

Before long, Confederate President Jefferson Davis replaced Johnston with the newly promoted General Hood, one of the Army of Tennessee's corps commanders. The combative Hood attacked Sherman repeatedly around Atlanta, which only reduced both the strength and effectiveness of his army. Ever impatient, Sherman resolved to achieve victory in time to assist U.S. President Abraham Lincoln's nomination to run for reelection that fall, and thus he made several unsuccessful attempts to force Hood out of Atlanta with Union cavalry raids designed to cut the one railroad still sustaining the city that Federal infantry had not already severed. Those raids all failed, and Hood himself responded by launching much of his cavalry to cut the Western & Atlantic RR well to the rear of Sherman's armies. That effort also failed. Sherman finally captured Atlanta by using his infantry to seize the last railroad supplying the Confederates

As vital as the railroads were to Sherman's logistics, he deeply appreciated how vital they were to Confederates, too—so when he wrecked railroads to prevent Confederates from using them, he wrecked them with thorough intensity. Sherman insisted that his troops not just bend heated rails, but twist them so they could not be reused without being recast. (dd)

defending the city, bringing the campaign to a successful close.

As Sherman rightly observed, "the great question of the campaign was one of supplies," and victory "would simply have been impossible without the use of the railroads from Louisville to Nashville . . . to Chattanooga . . . to Atlanta." The continuous operations (i.e., daily marching and fighting) that characterized the Atlanta campaign throughout its course resulted in the consumption of massive quantities of supplies by Sherman's army group. Union railroads in the area of operations, from November 1863 through September 1864, delivered a grand total of very nearly 300,000 tons of freight. The USMRR Construction Corps rebuilt 22.5 miles of track and more than 4,000 linear feet of bridges, used six million board feet of bridge timber and 500,000 cross ties, and spent $1.2 million on contract salaries.

Union quartermasters issued from the Nashville depot alone more than 4.7 million items as varied as shelter tents, infantry trousers, and canteens. For the whole campaign, Federal forces fired just over 22 million rounds of small-arms ammunition (overwhelmingly for the infantry's standard rifle-musket) and nearly 150,000 artillery rounds. To minimally feed all of Sherman's soldiers, horses, and mules each day required 850 tons of food and forage, which accounted for just over half the total tonnage of supplies arriving daily at Chattanooga.

In the end, uninterrupted logistics kept

Sherman's armies relentlessly grinding toward Atlanta, while denial of the same figured large in the Confederacy's loss of the city, which helped accomplish both Lincoln's reelection and the North's eventual triumph.

J. BRITT MCCARLEY, *Ph.D.,* *is Chief Historian for the U.S. Army Training and Doctrine Command (TRADOC), Ft. Eustis, VA, and is also Director of TRADOC's Military History and Heritage Program. He is a former historian with the National Park Service, where he worked at a variety of locations, including Kennesaw Mountain National Battlefield.*

Why do People Believe Joe Johnston Could Have Saved Atlanta?

APPENDIX E
BY STEPHEN DAVIS

To this day, a lot of students of the war consider Jefferson Davis' decision to relieve Gen. Joseph E. Johnston to have been a colossal mistake. They believe that, if he had been kept in command of the Army of Tennessee, Johnston could have held Atlanta till past the North's November election.

What's the basis of their belief?

It starts with what Joe Johnston himself claimed. The war was not even over—indeed, Hood's army had not yet marched out of Atlanta—when on September 1 Johnston wrote his friend Gen. Dabney Maury. "Just before I left the army," he asserted, "we thought the odds against us had been reduced almost six to four." On that basis he concluded, "I have not supposed therefore that Sherman could either invest Atlanta or carry it by assault." If he had been allowed to continue, Johnston went so far as to ask Maury, "is it not clear that we would soon have been able to give battle with abundant chances of victory, and that the enemy, beaten on this side of the Chattahoochee, would have been destroyed?"

Even before the end of the war, the Confederate press weighed in on the issue as well. Several weeks after the fall of Atlanta, the Montgomery *Mail* offered this opinion: "the evidence accumulates, that had Johnston been retained in command of the Tennessee army, Atlanta would not only have been saved, but Sherman's hosts would have been destroyed."

Opponents of President Davis railed against his decision to promote Hood and give him army command. One of the most outspoken was Texas Senator Louis T. Wigfall, a close friend of Joseph E. Johnston. In a Congressional report he issued less than a month before Robert E. Lee surrendered his army, Wigfall declared that Davis's decision in effect gave William T. Sherman a free pass. "In the effort to destroy Johnston," Wigfall announced, "the President saved Sherman from destruction."

Would that Joe Johnston could have kept Sherman out of Atlanta by posting a couple of signs at Tunnel Hill.... (dd)

For years after the war, Johnston held to his argument that his relief from command and Hood's appointment doomed Atlanta to enemy capture. There were variants in his message, though. One he expressed in an article published in the 1880s: "I assert that had one of the other lieutenant-generals of the army (Hardee or Stewart) succeeded me, Atlanta would have been held by the Army of Tennessee."

A decade after the war, Johnston used his memoirs to promulgate his contention that he could have saved Atlanta from enemy capture. In his *Narrative of Military Operations*, published in 1874, he argues that if he had been retained, "when the Federal army approached," he would have fallen back into the fortifications of Atlanta and committed defense of the city to Maj. Gen. Gustavus W. Smith's Georgia militia. Then, Johnston wrote, he planned to

> march out with the three corps against one of its flanks. If we were successful, the enemy would be driven against the Chattahoochee where there are no fords, or to the east, away from their communications, as the attack might fall on their right or left. If unsuccessful, the Confederate army had a near and secure place of refuge in Atlanta, which it could hold forever, and so win the campaign, of which that place was the object.

John B. Hood had begun collecting materials for his memoirs after the war, but the publication of Johnston's *Narrative* in 1874 speeded his work. He had finished his manuscript before his death in August 1879. Hood's *Advance and Retreat* was published by a memorial association the next year, and in it the author ridicules Johnston's boast. If he truly believed he could hold Atlanta "forever," why didn't he say so to Jefferson Davis when the president "was anxious to ascertain whether or not he intended to defend Atlanta"? Furthermore, Hood sarcastically reasons, if Johnston thought he could actually hold Atlanta "forever" in 1864, when he commanded in Virginia two years earlier, he surely should have also

Confederate defenses around Atlanta successfully held Federal armies at bay for months. George Barnard photographed this Confederate fort during the Federal occupation. The site today is that of the Fox Theatre in downtown Atlanta. (loc)

The Atlanta *Intelligencer* was the city's leading daily in 1864, bringing word of Sherman's approach to the city. It moved its presses to Macon after Johnston's army retreated across the Chattahoochee. (loc)

been able to hold Richmond "forever"—a feat, Hood notes, even the incomparable Lee could not achieve. Finally, after he was removed from command, Hood observes that Johnston left Atlanta so quickly "that I have almost been inclined to think he was rejoiced at having been relieved from the duty of holding Atlanta 'forever.'"

Brig. Gen. Arthur M. Manigault of South Carolina, who had served under both Johnston and Hood, supported Johnston in his memoirs, written several years after the war. "I have always thought that had General Johnston been permitted to retain the command," he asserted, "Sherman never would have gained Atlanta." Manigault stated his belief that if Johnston had been allowed to continue to battle Sherman on July 18 or 19, Johnston would not only "have defeated him and driven him across the river . . . but would have forced him to retire to Chattanooga."

Others extended Johnston's contention that if retained as army commander he could have saved Atlanta. In a speech delivered at the dedication of a monument to the general at Dalton in 1912, Moses H. Wright declared, "Had General Johnston been left in command, there would have been no march to the sea."

Some ex-Confederates, however, took Hood's side and disagreed with Johnston that if left in command he could have held Atlanta "forever." General Gustavus W. Smith, writing in the 1880s, picked apart Johnston's argument that Smith's militia could have defended the city while he took his army out of the fortifications to attack Sherman in flank. First, the state troops numbered only 2,000 at the time of Johnston's removal. "The Georgia militia were good fighters," Smith affirmed, but even in defensive works, "I do not think they could have held Atlanta." Finally, if he had been unsuccessful in his proposed attack and been compelled to fall back into the city's fortifications, Johnston gave "no assurance of his ability to prevent Sherman from turning the position, cutting off its railroad communications, and thus making it untenable for an army"—which, of course, was how Sherman eventually took the city from Hood.

One of the most extensive and enthusiastic defenses of Johnston appeared in a booklet written by Joseph M. Brown, son of Georgia's wartime governor, published in the late 1880s. "Could Johnston have Defended Atlanta Successfully?" was Brown's question, and he answered it forthrightly. "Let us suppose," he posited, that if General Johnston had been allowed to carry out his "programme,"

> the city would have been stubbornly and successfully defended. Sherman's lines of communication would have been constantly broken; his position would have been uncomfortable, if not perilous; and instead of Atlanta falling into the hands of the Federals... it would have been defended by Johnston until the first week of November. . . . This . . .would very seriously have endangered the republican party's chance of electing Lincoln, . . . and it is among the probabilities, if not a certainty, that McClellan would have been elected, in which event the war would have ended by reason of the confessed exhaustion of the north.

In short, Brown concluded, "Johnston's tactics

. . . would have ended the war with the independence of the Confederacy."

Since the passing of the war generation, historians have carried on the debate over what Johnston would have done if not relieved at Atlanta. Differing positions continue to be held seriously indeed. Perhaps it is well to take a step back, as Richard McMurry did in an essay published a few decades ago, in which he whimsically characterized Johnston's persistent supporters.

> *With a faith equaled only by that of Islamic zealots, they maintain that Davis removed their hero from the head of the army just as he was about to smite the Yankees hip and thigh. Had Johnston remained in command of the Army of Tennessee, they pontificate, he would have defeated Sherman, smashed the Federal army, chased the Unionists out of Georgia, driven them into Hudson Bay, and won victory and independence for the Confederacy.*

Well, maybe not quite, but you get the idea . . . .

In the second week of November, Sherman's commissary and quartermaster officers in Atlanta packed stores which would not be needed in the forthcoming march across Georgia. Trains were being loaded with the useless stuff and sent back north. Magnification of the wagon in midground shows a poster advertising a concert at the Atheneum on November 8. (loc)

What We've Learned about John Bell Hood Since the Centennial

APPENDIX F
BY STEPHEN DAVIS

Longevity has its place, Dr. King once said, and boy does it.

One of the pleasures of senescence—there are a few—is taking stock of how much one has learned over the years.

In the study of the Civil War, think about what we've learned just since the Centennial of 1961-65. We've discovered the Monitor off Cape Hatteras. We've found that the Hunley didn't go down with the Housatonic, but sank elsewhere in Charleston harbor; we've even been able to bury the sailors' remains in Magnolia Cemetery. We've learned that Robert E. Lee's last words were not "Strike the tent"; incapacitated by stroke, the General could not speak in his final hours.

We could go on. But here, my focus will be on the new stuff we've learned about the Atlanta campaign since I was a lad of 12 in April 1961, specifically about Confederate Gen. John B. Hood.

At that time, by my count, we had just two books on the Atlanta campaign (try counting them now). By far the better of them was Union Brig. Gen. Jacob D. Cox's *Atlanta* (1882), published in Scribner's "Campaigns of the Civil War" series. A thin, insubstantial effort was Atlanta newspaperman Bill Key's *The Battle of Atlanta and the Georgia Campaign* (1958).

Peachtree Creek, viewed from Peachtree Road bridge in Buckhead. Nearby, a memorial dedicated in 1935 commemorates "American Valor" in the Civil War and World War—with kepis and doughboy helmets chiseled in the stone. (dd)

Back in the Centennial, growing up in Atlanta, I recall that Joe Johnston owned this town. That is, most Civil War buffs here sided with Johnston in his many postwar arguments with Hood about the campaign.

Example is Key's statement that Hood "committed the unpardonable military sin" of going behind Johnston's back and sending the

Bill Key's book on the Atlanta campaign, the first modern study, filled in a gap but left much to be desired. (sd)

authorities in Richmond letters critical of his commander. Well, one of the things we've learned in the last half-century is that a whole lot of other Confederate officers were doing the same thing.

Thomas L. Connelly opened my eyes to this in his *Autumn of Glory* (1971). From the Braxton Bragg Papers at Cleveland's Western Reserve, Connelly discovered that Maj. Gen. Joe Wheeler secretly corresponded with Bragg. On July 1, 1864, he complained that General Johnston would not allow him to launch a raid into Sherman's rear to cut the Western & Atlantic Railroad.

So I looked into the Bragg Papers for myself (microfilm, University of Tennessee), and I saw still more officers had committed Hood's "unpardonable military sin." Generals Peter Stewart and Edward Walthall wrote Bragg in March. Stewart's missive was particularly biting. "Are we to hold still, remaining on the defensive in this position," he asked, until the Yankees came down with their "combined armies to drive us out?" Joseph Wheeler, meanwhile, sent Bragg four letters before the campaign even began.

What's more, the senior corps commander in Johnston's army got into the game. On June 22, with the army at Kennesaw Mountain, Lieutenant Gen. Hardee wrote the president, "if the present system continues we may find ourselves at Atlanta before a serious battle is fought." The letter is at Emory University; I don't see it in Nathaniel Hughes' biography of Hardee (1967). Since then, LSU's publication of The Papers of Jefferson Davis shows that Hardee wrote the president five letters in February '64 alone.

Sinners often excuse themselves with "but others did it too." With what we know today, criticism of Hood for writing Richmond has gradually subsided, if only because he was in such a large circle of brother officers doing the same thing.

Another aspect of our learning in recent years has to do with Johnston's and Hood's relationship. Fifty years ago, the literature emphasized the generals' bitter acrimony after the war, when both were writing their memoirs in the 1870s.

Today, however, a re-examination of the Atlanta campaign, as we've seen in this volume, leads one to see how often Johnston gave Hood—not Hardee—important tactical assignments, such as the flank attacks at Resaca and the maneuver at Cassville. At Kennesaw Mountain, when Sherman threatened to flank his left, Johnston sent Hood's corps to the threatened sector.

In another instance—one I don't mention in my main text—after the Federals were repulsed at Pickett's Mill, Johnston planned on May 28 to launch an attack of his own. Of course he gave the job to Hood, who that morning found that, during the night, the Yankees had shifted and strengthened their position, so he had to call it off.

With good reason, Hardee complained to his wife in a letter of June 20: "Hood, I think is helping the General to do the strategy, and from what I see is doing most of it." And recall that Johnston had Hood with him at his meeting with Senator Ben Hill on July 1 (Hardee wasn't there). Three weeks before he was about to be fired, Joe Johnston still leaned on John B. Hood.

Then there is Cassville. Up to the Centennial, most writers favored Johnston's claim that on May 19 Hood had been spooked by phantom troops. Govan and Livingood, Johnston's biographers (1956), assert that "Hood had incorrectly interpreted the situation," and that there were not enough Yankees out there for him to cancel his planned attack.

Since then things have shifted. "It can now be stated with certainty," Richard McMurry wrote in his doctoral dissertation at Emory for Bell Wiley (1967), "that there were Northern troops to the east of Hood's position." Albert Castel, in his monumental *Decision in the West* (1992) essentially ends the discussion by positing fully two divisions of Union cavalry (Ed McCook's and Stoneman's) bearing down on Hood's flank. Forcing Hood to cancel the Cassville flank attack, he writes, was "the most valuable service that will be performed by Sherman's cavalry during the entire campaign."

I've even contributed to the conversation, especially on what I call the "stupid, baseless derogation" that Hood was a junkie, resorting to laudanum or other opiates to manage some imagined postoperative pain from his wounds. Back in 1998 for

Johnston's memoir, *Narrative of Military Operations* (1874), spurred Hood to write a series of rebuttals in the *New Orleans Times*—a discovery I made two years ago at the Tulane Library. (loc)

Surely one of the most important "attic eurekas" occurred when Stephen M. Hood discovered a few years ago a previously unknown cache of letters, documents, and photographs possessed by Hood at the time of his death in 1879, and subsequently passed down to descendants. Sam Hood has used them in his two recent books about the general. (sb)

Blue & Gray, I went through the literature and found no writer who could prove the charge. Instead, I found a lot of speculation.

• Hood "may have been taking a derivative of laudanum" (McMurry, 1972)
    • "…especially if he took any liquor or a drug to relax" (McDonough and Connelly, 1983)
    • "perhaps swallowed some laudanum" (Sword, 1992)
    • Hood may have been impaired "perhaps from use of laudanum to dull his constant pain" (Garrison, 1995).

Other writers have jumped from maybe to did. "Hood suffered such intense pain that he was taking laudanum," Ronald Bailey asserts in his Time-Life book (1985). At Spring Hill, Craig Symonds writes that while Hood's hoped-for attack was falling apart, the general took "an early dinner and a laudanum-induced sleep" (*Stonewall Jackson of the West*, 1997).

Unfortunately one continues to see these slurs, but their frequency is happily dwindling. A real nail in the coffin of this libel was Stephen M. ("Sam") Hood's discovery in 2012 of a long-lost cache of General Hood's papers in the attic—I'm not kidding—of a descendant in Philadelphia. Among them was the medical log kept by Hood's physician, Dr. John Darby, in the weeks after Chickamauga and the general's leg amputation. Careful reading shows that Darby administered occasional, small doses of morphine to help Hood sleep, but that there was no chronic pain. Sam's perceptive article on these points, published in Civil War Times Illustrated in April 2015, led the editors to trumpet on their front cover, "Myth Busted!" Let's hope they're right.

So here's what we've learned:

Hood gets a sorta-pardon for writing over Johnston's head. Old Joe trusted Hood more than Hardee, and gave him the key responsibilities. Hood has won the argument over Cassville, and he was not an opium-eater.

Note too that I've just been discussing the campaign north of the Chattahoochee. What else may we expect to learn about Hood and the Atlanta campaign in the coming years? In our companion volume, *All the Fighting They Want*, when Hood commands the Army of Tennessee, we'll have even more to talk about.

ATLANTA CAMPAIGN,
MAY 5-JULY 18, 1864

MILITARY DIVISION OF THE MISSISSIPPI
Maj. Gen. William T. Sherman

Chief of Artillery: Brig. Gen. William F. Barry
Medical Director: Lt. Col. Edward D. Kittoe
Chief of Ordnance: Capt. Thomas G. Baylor
Chief Engineer: Capt. Orlando M. Poe
Headquarters Guard: *7th Company, Ohio Sharpshooters*

ARMY OF THE CUMBERLAND
Maj. Gen. George H. Thomas

Chief of Artillery: Brig. Gen. John M. Brannan
Medical Director: Surg. George E. Cooper
Chief Engineer: Lt. Henry C. Wharton
Chief of Ordnance: Lt. Otho F. Michaelis
Escort: *Co. I, 1st Ohio Cavalry*

FOURTH CORPS Maj. Gen. Oliver O. Howard
Chief of Artillery: Capt. Lyman Bridges

FIRST DIVISION: Maj. Gen. David S. Stanley
First Brigade: Maj. Gen. Charles Cruft; Col. Isaac M. Kirby
*21st Illinois • 38th Illinois • 31st Indiana • 81st Indiana • 1st Kentucky
2nd Kentucky • 90th Ohio • 101st Ohio*

Second Brigade: Brig. Gen. Walter C. Whitaker; Col. Jacob E. Taylor
96th Illinois • 115th Illinois • 35th Indiana • 21st Kentucky • 40th Ohio • 51st Ohio

Third Brigade: Col. William Grose; Col. P. Sidney Post
59th Illinois • 75th Indiana • 80th Illinois • 84th Illinois • 9th Indiana
30th Indiana • 36th Indiana • 84th Indiana • 77th Pennsylvania

Divisional Artillery: *Indiana Light, 5th Battery • Pennsylvania Light, Battery B*

SECOND DIVISION: Brig. Gen. John Newton
First Brigade: Col. Francis T. Sherman; Brig. Gen. Nathan Kimball
36th Illinois • 44th Illinois • 73rd Illinois • 74th Illinois • 88th Illinois
15th Missouri • 24th Wisconsin • 28th Kentucky

Second Brigade: Brig. Gen. George D. Wagner; Col. John W. Blake
100th Illinois • 40th Indiana • 57th Indiana • 26th Ohio • 97th Ohio
28th Kentucky

Third Brigade: Brig. Gen. Charles G. Harker; Brig. Gen. Luther P. Bradley
22nd Illinois • 27th Illinois • 42nd Illinois • 51st Illinois • 79th Illinois
3rd Kentucky • 64th Ohio • 65th Ohio • 125th Ohio

Divisional Artillery: *1st Illinois Light, Battery M • 1st Ohio Light, Battery A*

Third Division: Brig. Gen. Thomas J. Wood
First Brigade: Brig. Gen. August Willich; Col. William H. Gibson;
Col. Richard H. Nodine
25th Illinois • 35th Illinois • 89th Illinois • 32nd Indiana • 8th Kansas • 15th Ohio
49th Ohio • 15th Wisconsin

Second Brigade: Brig. Gen. William B. Hazen
59th Illinois • 6th Indiana • 5th Kentucky • 6th Kentucky • 23rd Kentucky • 1st Ohio
6th Ohio • 41st Ohio • 71st Ohio • 93rd Ohio • 124th Ohio

Third Brigade: Brig. Gen. Samuel Beatty; Col. Frederick Knefler
79th Indiana • 86th Indiana • 9th Kentucky • 17th Kentucky • 13th Ohio • 19th Ohio
59th Ohio

Divisional Artillery: *Illinois Light, Bridges's Battery • Ohio Light, 6th Battery*

FOURTEENTH CORPS Maj. Gen. John M. Palmer

FIRST DIVISION: Brig. Gen. Richard W. Johnson; Brig. Gen. John H. King

First Brigade: Brig. Gen William P. Carlin; Col. Anson G. McCook
104th Illinois • 42nd Indiana • 88th Indiana • 15th Kentucky • 2nd Ohio
33rd Ohio • 94th Ohio • 10th Wisconsin • 21st Wisconsin

Second Brigade: Brig. Gen. John H. King; Col. William Stoughton; Col. Marshall F. Moore
11th Michigan • 15th U. S. (6 companies Second Battalion) • 15th U. S. (9 companies First and Second Battalions) • 16th U. S. (4 companies First Battalion) • 16th U. S. (4 companies Second Battalion) • 18th U. S. (8 companies First and Third Battalions) 18th U. S. (Second Battalion) • 19th U. S. (First Battalion and A, Second Battalion)

Third Brigade: Col. Benjamin Scribner; Col. Josiah Given; Col. Marshall F. Moore
37th Indiana • 38th Indiana • 21st Ohio • 74th Ohio • 78th Pennsylvania 79th Pennsylvania • 1st Wisconsin

Divisional Artillery: *1st Illinois Light, Battery C • 1st Ohio Light, Battery I*

SECOND DIVISION: Brig. Gen Jefferson C. Davis
First Brigade: Brig. Gen. James D. Morgan
10th Illinois • 16th Illinois • 60th Illinois • 10th Michigan • 14th Michigan 17th New York

Second Brigade: Col. John G. Mitchell
34th Illinois • 78th Illinois • 98th Ohio • 108th Ohio • 113th Ohio • 121st Ohio

Third Brigade: Col. Daniel McCook; Col. Oscar F. Harmon; Col. Caleb J. Dilworth
85th Illinois • 86th Illinois • 110th Illinois • 125th Illinois • 22nd Indiana 52nd Ohio

Divisional Artillery: *2nd Illinois Light, Battery I • Wisconsin Light, 5th Battery*

THIRD DIVISION: Brig. Gen. Absalom Baird
First Brigade: Brig. Gen. John B. Turchin; Col. Moses B. Walker
19th Illinois • 24th Illinois • 82nd Indiana • 23rd Missouri • 11th Ohio • 17th Ohio 31st Ohio • 89th Ohio • 92nd Ohio

Second Brigade: Col. Ferdinand Van Derveer; Col. Newell Gleason
75th Indiana • 87th Indiana • 101st Indiana • 2nd Minnesota • 9th Ohio 35th Ohio • 105th Ohio

Third Brigade: Col. George P. Este
10th Indiana • 74th Indiana • 10th Kentucky • 18th Kentucky • 14th Ohio 38th Ohio

Divisional Artillery: *Indiana Light, 7th Battery; Indiana Light, 19th Battery*

TWENTIETH CORPS: Maj. Gen. Joseph Hooker

FIRST DIVISION: Brig. Gen. Alpheus S. Williams
First Brigade: Brig. Gen. Joseph F. Knipe
*5th Connecticut • 3rd Maryland Detachment • 123rd New York • 141st New York
46th Pennsylvania*

Second Brigade: Brig. Gen. Thomas H. Ruger
*27th Indiana • 2nd Massachusetts • 13th New Jersey • 107th New York
150th New York • 3rd Wisconsin*

Third Brigade: Col. James S. Robinson
82nd Illinois • 101st Illinois • 45th New York • 143rd New York • 61st Ohio • 82nd Ohio

Divisional Artillery: *1st New York Light, Battery I • 1st New York Light, Battery M*

SECOND DIVISION: Brig. Gen. John W. Geary
First Brigade: Col. Charles Candy
5th Ohio • 7th Ohio • 29th Ohio • 66th Ohio • 28th Pennsylvania • 147th Pennsylvania

Second Brigade: Col. Adolphus Buschbeck; Col. John T. Lockman; Col.
Patrick H. Jones
*33rd New Jersey • 119th New York • 134th New York • 154th New York
27th Pennsylvania • 73rd Pennsylvania • 109th Pennsylvania*

Third Brigade: Col. David Ireland; Col. George A. Cobham
*60th New York • 78th New York • 102nd New York • 137th New York
149th New York • 29th Pennsylvania • 111th Pennsylvania*

Divisional Artillery: *New York Light, 13th Battery; Pennsylvania Light, Battery E*

THIRD DIVISION: Maj. Gen Daniel Butterfield; Brig. Gen William T. Ward
First Brigade: Brig. Gen William T. Ward; Col. Benjamin Harrison
102nd Illinois • 105th Illinois • 129th Illinois • 70th Indiana • 79th Ohio

Second Brigade: Col. John Coburn
20th Connecticut • 33rd Indiana • 85th Indiana • 19th Michigan • 22nd Wisconsin

Third Brigade: Col. James Wood
*20th Connecticut • 33rd Massachusetts • 136th New York • 55th Ohio • 73rd Ohio
26th Wisconsin*

Reserve Brigade: Col. Joseph W. Burke; Col. Heber Le Favour
10th Ohio • 9th Michigan • 22nd Michigan

Divisional Artillery: *1st Michigan Light, Battery I • 1st Ohio Light, Battery C*

Pontoniers: Col. George P. Buell
58th Indiana • Pontoon Battalion
Ammunition Train Guard: Capt. Gershom M. Barber
1st Battalion Ohio Sharpshooters
Siege Artillery: Capt. Arnold Sutermeister
11th Indiana Battery

CAVALRY CORPS: Brig. Gen. Washington Elliott

FIRST DIVISION: Brig. Gen. Edward M. McCook
First Brigade: Col. Joseph B. Dorr
8th Iowa • 4th Kentucky Mounted Infantry • 2nd Michigan • 1st Tennessee

Second Brigade: Col. Oscar H. LaGrange; Lt. Col. James W. Stewart;
Lt. Col. Horace P. Lamson
2nd Indiana • 4th Indiana • 1st Wisconsin

Third Brigade: Col. Louis D. Watkins; Col. John K. Faulkner
4th Kentucky • 6th Kentucky • 7th Kentucky

Divisional Artillery: *18th Indiana Battery*

SECOND DIVISION: Brig. Gen. Kenner Garrard
First Brigade: Col. Robert H. G. Minty
4th Michigan • 7th Pennsylvania • 4th U. S.

Second Brigade: Col. Eli Long
1st Ohio • 3rd Ohio • 4th Ohio

Third Brigade (Mounted Infantry): Col. John T. Wilder; Col. Abram O.
Miller
98th Illinois • 123rd Illinois • 17th Indiana • 72nd Indiana

Divisional Artillery: *Chicago Board of Trade Battery*

THIRD DIVISION: Brig. Gen. Judson Kilpatrick; Col. Eli H. Murray;
Col. William W. Lowe

First Brigade: Lt. Col. Robert Klein
3rd Indiana • 5th Iowa

Second Brigade: Col. Charles C. Smith; Maj. Thomas W. Sanderson
8th Indiana • 2nd Kentucky • 10th Ohio

Third Brigade: Col. Eli H. Murray; Col. Smith D. Adkins
92nd Illinois Mounted Infantry • 3rd Kentucky • 5th Kentucky

Divisional Artillery: *10thWisconsin Battery*

ARMY OF THE TENNESSEE
Maj. Gen. James B. McPherson

Chief of Artillery: Capt. Andrew Hickenlooper
Medical Director: Surgeon John Moore
Chief Engineer: Capt. Chauncey B. Reese

FIFTEENTH CORPS: Maj. Gen. John A. Logan
FIRST DIVISION: Brig. Gen. Peter J. Osterhaus; Brig. Gen. Charles R. Woods
First Brigade: Brig. Gen. Charles R. Woods
26th Iowa • 30th Iowa • 27th Missouri • 76th Ohio

Second Brigade: Col. James A. Williamson
4th Iowa • 9th Iowa • 25th Iowa • 31st Iowa

Third Brigade: Col. Hugo Wangelin
*3rd Missouri • 12th Missouri • 17th Missouri • 29th Missouri • 31st Missouri •
32nd Missouri*

Divisional Artillery: *2nd Missouri Light, Battery F • Ohio Light, 4th Battery*

SECOND DIVISION: Brig. Gen. Morgan L. Smith
First Brigade: Brig. Gen. Giles A. Smith
*55th Illinois • 111th Illinois • 116th Illinois • 127th Illinois • 6th Missouri •
8th Missouri • 30th Ohio • 57th Ohio*

Second Brigade: Brig. Gen. Joseph Lightburn
*111th Illinois • 83rd Indiana • 30th Ohio • 37th Ohio • 47th Ohio • 53rd Ohio •
54th Ohio*

Divisional Artillery: Capt. Francis DeGress
1st Illinois Light, Battery A • 1st Illinois Light, Battery B • 1st Illinois Light, Battery H

THIRD DIVISION: Brig. Gen. William Harrow
First Brigade: Col. Reuben Williams
*26th Illinois • 48th Illinois • 90th Illinois • 12th Indiana • 99th Indiana
100th Indiana • 15th Michigan • 70th Ohio*

Second Brigade: Brig. Gen. Charles C. Walcutt
40th Illinois • 103rd Illinois • 97th Indiana • 6th Iowa • 46th Ohio

Third Brigade: Col. John M. Oliver
48th Illinois • 99th Indiana • 15th Michigan • 70th Ohio

Divisional Artillery: Capt. Henry H. Griffiths; Maj. John T. Cheney
1st Illinois Light, Battery F • Iowa Light, 1st Battery

SIXTEENTH CORPS: Maj. Gen. Grenville M. Dodge

SECOND DIVISION: Brig. Gen. Thomas W. Sweeny
First Brigade: Brig. Gen. Elliott W. Rice
52nd Illinois • 66th Indiana • 2nd Iowa • 7th Iowa

Second Brigade: Col. Patrick E. Burke; Lt. Col. Robert N. Adams; Col. August Mersy
9th Illinois Mounted Infantry • 12th Illinois • 66th Illinois • 81st Ohio

Third Brigade: Col. Moses E. Bane
7th Illinois • 50th Illinois • 57th Illinois • 39th Iowa

Divisional Artillery: Capt. Frederick Welker
1st Michigan Light, Battery B • 1st Missouri Light, Battery H • 1st Missouri Light, Battery I

FOURTH DIVISION: Brig. Gen. James C. Veatch; Brig. Gen. John W. Fuller
First Brigade: Brig. Gen. John W. Fuller
64th Illinois • 18th Missouri • 27th Ohio • 39th Ohio

Second Brigade: Brig. Gen. John W. Sprague
35th New Jersey • 43rd Ohio • 63rd Ohio • 25th Wisconsin

Third Brigade: Col. William T. C. Grower
10th Illinois • 25th Indiana • 17th New York • 32nd Wisconsin

Divisional Artillery: Capt. Jerome B. Burrows; Capt. George Robinson
1st Michigan Light, Battery C • Ohio Light, 14th Battery • 2nd U. S., Battery F

SEVENTEENTH ARMY CORPS: Maj. Gen. Francis P. Blair

THIRD DIVISION: Brig. Gen. Mortimer D. Leggett
First Brigade: Brig. Gen. Manning F. Force
20th Illinois • 30th Illinois • 31st Illinois • 12th Wisconsin • 16th Wisconsin

Second Brigade: Col. Robert K. Scott
20th Ohio • 32nd Ohio • 68th Ohio • 78th Ohio

Third Brigade: Col. Adam G. Malloy
17th Wisconsin • Worden's Battalion

Divisional Artillery: Capt. William S. Williams
1st Illinois Light, Battery D • 1st Michigan Light, Battery H • Ohio Light, 3rd Battery

FOURTH DIVISION: Brig. Gen. Walter Q. Gresham
First Brigade: Col. William L. Sanderson
32nd Illinois • 53rd Illinois • 23rd Indiana • 53rd Indiana • 3rd Iowa (3 companies)
32nd Ohio • 12th Wisconsin

Second Brigade: Col. George C. Rogers; Col. Isaac C. Pugh
14th Illinois • 15th Illinois • 32nd Illinois • 41st Illinois • 53rd Illinois

Third Brigade: Col. William Hall
11th Iowa • 13th Iowa • 15th Iowa • 16th Iowa

Divisional Artillery: Capt. Edward Spear
2nd Illinois Light, Battery F • Minnesota Light, 1st Battery • 1st Missouri Light, Battery C
Ohio Light, 10th Battery • Ohio Light, 15th Battery

ARMY OF THE OHIO
Maj. Gen. John M. Schofield

TWENTY-THIRD CORPS: Maj. Gen. Jacob D. Cox

FIRST DIVISION: Brig. Gen. Alvin P. Hovey
First Brigade: Col. Richard Barter
120th Indiana • 124th Indiana • 128th Indiana

Second Brigade: Col. John Q. McQuiston; Col. Peter T. Swaine
123rd Indiana • 129th Indiana • 130th Indiana • 99th Ohio

Divisional Artillery: *Indiana Light, 23rd Battery • Indiana Light, 24th Battery*

SECOND DIVISION: Brig. Gen. Henry M. Judah; Brig. Gen Milo S. Hascall
First Brigade: Brig. Gen. Nathaniel C. McLean; Brig. Gen. Joseph A. Cooper
80th Indiana • 91st Indiana • 13th Kentucky • 25th Michigan • 45th Ohio
3rd Tennessee • 6th Tennessee

Second Brigade: Brig. Gen. Milo S. Hascall; Col. John R. Bond; Col. William E. Hobson
107th Illinois • 80th Indiana • 13th Kentucky • 23rd Michigan • 45th Ohio
111th Ohio • 118th Ohio

Third Brigade: Col. Silas A. Strickland
14th Kentucky • 20th Kentucky • 27th Kentucky • 50th Ohio

Divisional Artillery: Capt. Joseph C. Shields
Indiana Light, 22nd Battery • 1st Michigan Light, Battery F • Ohio Light, 19th Battery

THIRD DIVISION: Brig. Gen. Jacob D. Cox; Col. James W. Reilly
First Brigade: Col. James W. Reilly; Maj. James W. Gault
112th Illinois • 16th Kentucky • 100th Ohio • 104th Ohio • 8th Tennessee

Second Brigade: Brig. Gen. Mahlon D. Manson; Col. John S. Hurt;
Col. Milo S. Hascall; Col. John S. Casement; Col. Daniel Cameron
65th Illinois • 63rd Indiana • 65th Indiana • 24th Kentucky • 103rd Ohio • 5th Tennessee

Third Brigade: Brig. Gen. Nathaniel McLean; Col. Robert K. Byrd
11th Kentucky • 12th Kentucky • 1st Tennessee • 5th Tennessee

Dismounted Cavalry Brigade: Col. Eugene W. Crittenden
16th Illinois • 12th Kentucky

Divisional Artillery: Maj. Henry W. Wells
Indiana Light, 15th Battery • 1st Ohio Light, Battery D

STONEMAN'S CAVALRY DIVISION: Maj. Gen. George Stoneman
First Brigade: Col. Israel Garrard
9th Michigan • 7th Ohio

Second Brigade: Col. James Biddle
16th Illinois • 5th Indiana • 6th Indiana • 12th Kentucky

Third Brigade: Col. Horace Capron
14th Illinois • 8th Michigan • McLaughlin's Ohio Squadron

Independent Brigade: Col. Alexander W. Holeman
1st Kentucky • 11th Kentucky

Divisional Artillery: Capt. Alexander Hardy
24th Indiana Battery

ARMY OF TENNESSEE
Gen. Joseph E. Johnston

Chief of Staff: Brig. Gen. William W. Mackall
Chief of Artillery: Brig. Gen. Francis A. Shoup
Chief Engineer: Lt. Col. Stephen W. Presstman
Medical Director: Surg.-Maj. A.J. Foard

HARDEE'S CORPS: Lt. Gen. William J. Hardee

CHEATHAM'S DIVISION: Maj. Gen. Benjamin F. Cheatham

Maney's Brigade: Brig. Gen. George E. Maney; Col. Francis M. Walker
*1st & 27th Tennessee • 4th Confederate • 6th & 9th Tennessee • 41st Tennessee
50th Tennessee • 24th Tennessee Battalion*

Strahl's Brigade: Brig. Gen. Otho F. Strahl
4th & 5th Tennessee • 19th Tennessee • 24th Tennessee • 31st Tennessee • 33rd Tennessee

Wright's Brigade: Col. John C. Carter
8th Tennessee • 16th Tennessee • 28th Tennessee • 38th Tennessee • 51st & 52nd Tennessee

Vaughan's Brigade: Brig. Gen. Alfred J. Vaughan; Col. Michael Magevney
11th Tennessee • 12th & 47th Tennessee • 29th Tennessee • 13th & 154th Tennessee

CLEBURN'S DIVISION: Maj. Gen. Patrick R. Cleburne

Polk's Brigade: Brig. Gen. Lucius E. Polk
*1st & 15th Arkansas • 5th Confederate • 2nd Tennessee • 35th Tennessee
48th Tennessee (Nixon's regiment)*

Govan's Brigade: Brig. Gen. Daniel C. Govan
*2nd & 24th Arkansas • 5th & 13th Arkansas • 6th & 7th Arkansas
8th & 19th Arkansas • 3rd Confederate*

Lowrey's Brigade: Brig. Gen. Mark P. Lowrey
16th Alabama • 33rd Alabama • 45th Alabama • 32nd Mississippi • 45th Mississippi

Granbury's Brigade: Brig. Gen. Hiram B. Granbury
*6th Texas • 7th Texas • 10th Texas • 15th Texas Cavalry (dismounted)
17th & 18th Texas Cavalry (dismounted) • 24th & 25th Texas Cavalry (dismounted)*

BATE'S DIVISION: Maj. Gen. William B. Bate
Tyler's Brigade: Brig. Gen. Thomas B. Smith
37th Georgia • 4th Georgia Battalion Sharpshooters • 10th Tennessee • 20th Tennessee
30th Tennessee • 15th & 37th Tennessee

Lewis's Brigade: Brig. Gen. Joseph H. Lewis
2nd Kentucky • 4th Kentucky • 5th Kentucky • 6th Kentucky • 9th Kentucky

Finley's Brigade: Brig. Gen. Jesse J. Finley
1st Florida Calvary (dismounted) • 1st & 4th Florida • 3rd Florida • 6th Florida • 7th Florida

WALKER'S DIVISION: Maj. Gen. William H. T. Walker
Mercer's Brigade: Brig. Gen. Hugh W. Mercer
1st Volunteer Georgia • 54th Georgia • 57th Georgia • 63rd Georgia

Gist's Brigade: Brig. Gen. States R. Gist
8th Georgia Battalion • 46th Georgia • 16th South Carolina • 24th South Carolina

Jackson's Brigade: Brig. Gen. John K. Jackson
1st Georgia Confederate • 5th Georgia • 47th Georgia • 65th Georgia • 5th Mississippi
• 8th Mississippi • 2nd Georgia Battalion Sharpshooters

Stevens's Brigade: Brig. Gen. Clement H. Stevens
25th Georgia • 29th Georgia • 30th Georgia • 66th Georgia • 1st Georgia Battalion
Sharpshooters • 26th Georgia Battalion

HARDEE'S CORPS ARTILLERY: Col. Melancthon Smith
Hoxton's Battalion: Maj. Llewelyn Hoxton
Alabama Battery • Marion (Florida) Light Artillery • Mississippi Battery

Hotchkiss's Battalion: Maj. Thomas R. Hotchkiss
Arkansas Battery • Semple's (Alabama) Battery • Warren (Mississippi) Light Artillery

Martin's Battalion: Maj. Robert Martin
Bledsoe's (Missouri) Battery • Ferguson's (South Carolina) Battery • Howell's (Georgia) Battery

Cobb's Battalion: Maj. Robert Cobb
Cobb's (Kentucky) Battery • Johnston (Tennessee) Artillery • Washington (Louisiana) Light Artillery

HOOD'S CORPS: Lt. Gen. John B. Hood

HINDMAN'S DIVISION: Maj. Gen. Thomas C. Hindman; Brig. Gen. John C. Brown

Deas's Brigade: Brig. Gen. Zachariah C. Deas
19th Alabama • 22nd Alabama • 25th Alabama • 39th Alabama • 50th Alabama
17th Alabama Battalion Sharpshooters

Manigault's Brigade: Brig. Gen. Arthur M. Manigault
24th Alabama • 28th Alabama • 34th Alabama • 10th South Carolina • 19th South Carolina

Walthall's Brigade: Brig. Gen. Edward C. Walthall; Col. Samuel Benton
24th & 27th Mississippi • 29th, 30th and 34th Mississippi

Tucker's Brigade: Brig. Gen. William F. Tucker; Col. Jacob H. Sharp
7th Mississippi • 9th Mississippi • 10th Mississippi • 41st Mississippi
44th Mississippi • 9th Mississippi Battalion Sharpshooters

STEVENSON'S DIVISION: Maj. Gen. Carter L. Stevenson
Brown's Brigade: Brig. Gen. John C. Brown; Col. Joseph C. Palmer
3rd Tennessee • 18th Tennessee • 26th Tennessee • 32nd Tennessee
45th & 23rd Tennessee Battalion

Cumming's Brigade: Brig. Gen. Alfred Cumming
34th Georgia • 36th Georgia • 39th Georgia • 56th Georgia

Reynolds's Brigade: Brig. Gen. Alexander W. Reynolds
58th North Carolina • 60th North Carolina • 54th Virginia • 63rd Virginia

Pettus's Brigade: Brig. Gen. Edmund W. Pettus
20th Alabama • 23rd Alabama • 30th Alabama • 31st Alabama • 46th Alabama

STEWART'S DIVISION: Maj. Gen. Alexander P. Stewart; Maj. Gen. Henry D. Clayton
Stovall's Brigade: Brig. Gen. Marcellus A. Stovall; Col. Abda Johnson
40th Georgia • 41st Georgia • 42nd Georgia • 43rd Georgia • 52nd Georgia

Clayton's Brigade: Brig. Gen. Henry D. Clayton; Brig. Gen. James T. Holtzclaw
18th Alabama • 32nd & 58th Alabama • 36th Alabama • 38th Alabama

Gibson's Brigade: Brig. Gen .Randall L. Gibson
1st Louisiana • 13th Louisiana • 16th & 25th Louisiana • 19th Louisiana
20th Louisiana • 4th Louisiana Battalion • 14th Louisiana Battalion Sharpshooters

Baker's Brigade: Brig. Gen. Alpheus Baker
37th Alabama • 40th Alabama • 42nd Alabama

HOOD'S CORPS ARTILLERY: Col. Robert F. Beckham
Courtney's Battalion: Maj. Alfred R. Courtney
Alabama Battery • Douglas's (Texas) Battery • Alabama Battery

Eldridge's Battalion: Maj. John W. Eldridge
Eufaula (Alabama) Artillery • Louisiana Battery • Mississippi Battery

Johnston's Battalion: Maj. John W. Johnston; Cap. Max. Van Den Corput
Cherokee (Georgia) Artillery • Stephens (Georgia) Light Artillery • Tennessee Battery

ARMY OF TENNESSEE ARTILLERY RESERVE

Palmer's Battalion: Maj. Joseph Palmer
Georgia Battery • Alabama Battery • Georgia Battery

Williams' Battalion: Lt. Col. Samuel C. Williams
Barbour (Alabama) Artillery • Jefferson (Mississippi) Artillery • Nottoway (Virginia) Artillery

Waddell's Battalion: Maj. James F. Waddell
Emery's (Alabama) Battery • Bellamy's (Alabama) Battery • Barret's (Missouri) Battery

CAVALRY CORPS: Maj. Gen ,Joseph Wheeler

MARTIN'S DIVISION: Maj. Gen. William T. Martin
Morgan's Brigade: Brig. Gen. John T. Morgan
1st Alabama • 3rd Alabama • 4th Alabama • 7th Alabama • 51st Alabama

Iverson's Brigade: Brig. Gen. Alfred Iverson
1st Georgia • 2nd Georgia • 3rd Georgia • 4th Georgia • 6th Georgia

KELLY'S DIVISION: Brig. Gen. John H. Kelly
Allen's Brigade: Brig. Gen. William W. Allen
3rd Confederate • 8th Confederate • 10th Confederate • 12th Confederate

Dibrell's Brigade: Col. George G. Dibrell
4th Tennessee • 8th Tennessee • 9th Tennessee • 10th Tennessee • 11th Tennessee

Williams' Brigade: Brig. Gen John S. Williams
*1st Kentucky • 2nd Kentucky • 9th Kentucky • 2nd Kentucky Battalion
Allison's (Tennessee) Squadron • detachment Hamilton's (Tennessee) Battalion*

Hannon's Brigade: Col. Moses W. Hannon
53rd Alabama • 24th Alabama Battalion

HUMES'S DIVISION: Brig Gen. William Y. C. Humes
Humes's Brigade: Col. James T. Wheeler
1st Tennessee • 2nd Tennessee • 5th Tennessee • 9th Tennessee Battalion

Harrison's Brigade: Col. Thomas H. Harrison
3rd Arkansas • 8th Texas • 11th Texas

CAVALRY CORPS ARTILLERY: Lt. Col. Felix H. Robertson
Ferrell's (Georgia) Battery (1 section) • Huwald's (Tennessee) Battery • Tennessee Battery Wiggins' (Arkansas) Battery

ARMY OF MISSISSIPPI
Lt. Gen. Leonidas Polk
Maj. Gen. William W. Loring
Maj. Gen. Alexander P. Stewart

Chief of Artillery: Lt. Col. Samuel C. Williams

LORING'S DIVISION: Maj. Gen. William W. Loring; Brig. Gen. Winfield S. Featherston
Featherston's Brigade: Brig. Gen. Winfield S. Featherston
3rd Mississippi • 22nd Mississippi • 31st Mississippi • 33rd Mississippi 40th Mississippi • 1st Mississippi Battalion Sharpshooters

Adams's Brigade: Brig. Gen. John Adams
6th Mississippi • 14th Mississippi • 15th Mississippi • 20th Mississippi 23rd Mississippi • 43rd Mississippi

Scott's Brigade: Brig. Gen. Thomas M. Scott
27th Alabama • 35th Alabama • 49th Alabama • 55th Alabama • 57th Alabama 12th Louisiana

Divisional Artillery/Myrick's Battalion: Maj. John D. Myrick
Mississippi Battery • Lookout Tennessee Battery • Pointe Coupee Battery

FRENCH'S DIVISION: Maj. Gen. Samuel G. French
Ector's Brigade: Brig. Gen. Mathew D. Ector
29th North Carolina • 39th North Carolina • 9th Texas • 10th Texas Cavalry (dismounted) 14th Texas Cavalry (dismounted) • 32nd Texas Cavalry (dismounted)

Cockrell's Brigade: Brig. Gen. Francis M. Cockrell; Col. Elijah Gates
1st & 4th Missouri • 2nd & 6th Missouri • 3rd & 5th Missouri 1st & 3rd Missouri Cavalry (dismounted)

Sears' Brigade: Brig. Gen. Claudius W. Sears
*4th Mississippi • 35th Mississippi • 36th Mississippi • 46th Mississippi
7th Mississippi Battalion*

Divisional Artillery/Storrs' Battalion: Maj. George S. Storrs
Ward's (Alabama) Battery • Hoskins' (Mississippi) Battery • Guibor's (Missouri) Battery

WALTHALL'S DIVISION: Maj. Gen. Edward C. Walthall
Reynolds' Brigade: Brig. Gen. Daniel H. Reynolds
*1st Arkansas Mounted Rifles (dismounted) • 2nd Arkansas Mounted Rifles (dismounted)
4th Arkansas • 9th Arkansas • 25th Arkansas*

Cantey's Brigade: Brig. Gen. James Cantey; Col. Edward A. O'Neal
*17th Alabama • 26th Alabama • 29th Alabama • 37th Mississippi
Battalion Alabama Sharpshooters*

Quarles' Brigade: Brig. Gen. William A. Quarles
*1st Alabama • 4th Alabama • 30th Louisiana • 42nd Tennessee • 46th & 55th Tennessee
48th Tennessee • 49th Tennessee • 53rd Tennessee*

Divisional Artillery/Preston's Battalion: Maj. William C. Preston
Yates's (Mississippi) Battery • Tarrant's (Alabama) Battery • Selden's (Alabama) Battery

CAVALRY DIVISION: Brig. Gen. William H. Jackson
Armstrong's Brigade: Brig. Gen. Frank C. Armstrong
1st Mississippi • 2nd Mississippi • 28th Mississippi • Ballentine's (Mississippi) Regiment

Ross' Brigade: Brig. Gen. Lawrence S. Ross
3rd Texas • 6th Texas • 9th Texas • 1st Texas Legion

Ferguson's Brigade: Brig. Gen. Samuel W. Ferguson
2nd Alabama • 56th Alabama • 9th Mississippi • 11th Mississippi • 12th Mississippi Battalion

Divisional Artillery: Capt. John Waties
Columbus (Georgia) Light Artillery • Clark (Missouri) Artillery • Waties' (South Carolina) Battery

ENGINEER TROOPS: Maj. Stephen W. Presstman
Companies A-D, F, G • Sappers & Miners

GEORGIA MILITIA (FIRST DIVISION)
Maj. Gen. Gustavus W. Smith

First Brigade: Brig. Gen. Reuben W. Carswell
1st Regiment • 2nd Regiment • 3rd Regiment

Second Brigade: Brig. Gen. Pleasant J. Philips
4th Regiment • 5th Regiment • 6th Regiment

Third Brigade: Brig. Gen. Charles D. Anderson
7th Regiment • 8th Regiment • 9th Regiment

Fourth Brigade: Brig. Gen. Henry K. McCay
10th Regiment • 11th Regiment • 12th Regiment

Suggested Reading

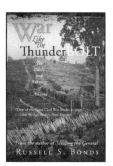

War Like the Thunderbolt: The Battle and Burning of Atlanta
Russell S. Bonds
Westholme Publishing
ISBN: 1594161275 (paperback)

A gracefully written narrative, synthesizing all the major sources in the campaign literature.

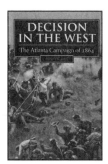

Decision in the West: The Atlanta Campaign of 1864
Albert Castel
University Press of Kansas (1992)
ISBN: 978-0-7006-0748-8 (paperback)

Absolutely the best book on the campaign. Scholarly, detailed, balanced. Albert once told me he initially thought of continuing his narrative to include Sherman's march to the sea. But with the Union occupation of Atlanta, he had so much material (the book is 665 pages!) that he stopped on Sept. 2, 1864.

Atlanta Will Fall: Sherman, Joe Johnston, and the Yankee Heavy Battalions
Stephen Davis
Rowman Littlefield (2001)
ISBN: 0-8420-2788-2 (paperback)

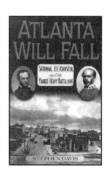

Immodesty alert: when Prof. Steven Woodworth invited me to write a book on the Atlanta campaign, I jumped. Publisher's constraints restricted my narrative, but I made my main points. Included in them was that Henry Watterson, veteran journalist, wrote for his paper two weeks into the campaign that he believed Atlanta would fall. (It did.) I draw from my research and writing for this volume for the Emerging Civil War Series.

Marching through Georgia: The Story of Soldiers and Civilians During Sherman's Campaign.
Lee Kennett
HarperCollins (1995)
ISBN: 978-0-0609-2745-5 (paperback)

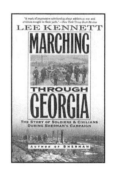

Not a military history like Castel's and McMurry's, Lee Kennett offers a useful complement. He describes his book as an attempt to recapture the collective experiences "of soldiers and civilians caught up in one of the Civil War's most celebrated campaigns." Lee's research in manuscript libraries, allowing him to quote from countless soldiers' writings, alone ranks this volume among the highest.

Atlanta 1864: Last Chance for the Confederacy
Richard M. McMurry
University of Nebraska Press (2000)
ISBN: 978-0-8032-8278-0 (paperback)

Richard has been a lifelong student of the Atlanta campaign. He wrote his doctoral dissertation on its first phase under Prof. Bell Wiley in 1965. This work demonstrates what I call Dr. McMurry's trademark concision. For a shorter narrative than Castel, there is none better than this.

About the Author

Steve Davis of Atlanta has been a Civil War buff since the fourth grade. He attended Emory University and studied under the renowned Civil War historian Bell Wiley. After a master's degree in American history from the University of North Carolina at Chapel Hill, he taught high school for a few years, then earned his Ph.D. at Emory, where he concentrated on the theme of the Civil War in Southern literature.

Steve is the author of an in-depth book on the Atlanta campaign, *Atlanta Will Fall: Sherman, John Johnston and the Heavy Yankee Battalions* (2001). His book *What the Yankees Did to Us: Sherman's Bombardment and Wrecking of Atlanta* was published by Mercer University Press in 2012. In a review in *Civil War News*, Ted Savas calls Steve's book "by far the most well-researched, thorough, and detailed account ever written about the 'wrecking' of Atlanta."

Steve served as Book Review Editor for *Blue & Gray* magazine from 1984 to 2005, and is the author of more than a hundred articles in such scholarly and popular publications as *Civil War Times Illustrated* and the *Georgia Historical Quarterly*. He also served as the historian/content partner for the Civil War Trust's Atlanta Campaign Battle App, produced in 2013-14.

In 2015, Steve served as a speaker and consultant for the television documentary "When Georgia Howled: Sherman on the March," a joint production of the Atlanta History Center and Georgia Public Broadcasting. Steve is also a popular speaker to Civil War round tables and historical societies. His favorite event was a couple of years ago when he addressed President and Mrs. Carter and family on the role of Copenhill (the Carter Center) in the battle of Atlanta.

Steve is author of a companion volume to this book, also part of the Emerging Civil War Series:

All the Fighting They Want: The Atlanta Campaign
From Peach Tree Creek to the Surrender
July 18-September 2, 1864

EMERGING CIVIL WAR SERIES